Professional Practice in Child Protection and the Child's Right to Participate

This book explains and discusses how a child's right to freedom of expression is upheld through practice and decision-making in Child Protection Services (CPS).

Using the right to expression as stipulated in Article 12.2 of the United Nations Convention on the Rights of the Child (CRC) as a point of departure, it explains what CPS practices should look like and how they must operate to uphold and enforce the rights of the child by providing "the opportunity to be heard" in any administrative practice. Current research literature documents extensively, and across countries, how either the voice of the child is not heard or, alternatively, the existence of a pro forma/ tokenistic approach to listening to the child throughout CPS practices. Taking a three-fold approach, this book

- establishes a clearer connection between rights and professional practice according to Article 12
- extrapolates how rights-based practice is achieved during CPS practices
- provides a comprehensive answer to the challenge of implementing Article 12.2 through policy and legislation.

It will be of interest to all students, academic and professionals working within child protection including social workers, probation officers, health and social care workers, lawyers and teachers.

Asgeir Falch-Eriksen is head of the academic unit Globalization and Social Sustainability at the Department of Social Work, Child Welfare and Social Policy at Oslo Metropolitan University. He also holds a position as associate professor at the Centre for Discretion and Paternalism (DIPA) at the University of Bergen. He has a PhD in political science and specializes in political theory, legal philosophy and the sociology of the professions. He has published multiple articles on professionalism in child protection and on the interconnection between child protection and human rights.

Karmen Toros is a professor of Social Work at the School of Governance, Law and Society, Tallinn University. She is actively involved in social work education and training of child protection workers. Her research focuses on child welfare and protection, strengths-perspective and solution-focused approach in child protection practice and is particularly interested in child protection assessment of children in need.

Professional Practice in Child Protection and the Child's Right to Participate

Edited by
Asgeir Falch-Eriksen and
Karmen Toros

Routledge
Taylor & Francis Group
LONDON AND NEW YORK

First published 2023
by Routledge
4 Park Square, Milton Park, Abingdon, Oxon OX14 4RN

and by Routledge
605 Third Avenue, New York, NY 10158

Routledge is an imprint of the Taylor & Francis Group, an informa business

© 2023 selection and editorial matter, Asgeir Falch-Eriksen and Karmen Toros; individual chapters, the contributors

The right of Asgeir Falch-Eriksen and Karmen Toros to be identified as the authors of the editorial material, and of the authors for their individual chapters, has been asserted in accordance with sections 77 and 78 of the Copyright, Designs and Patents Act 1988.

British Library Cataloguing-in-Publication Data
A catalogue record for this book is available from the British Library

Library of Congress Cataloging-in-Publication Data
A catalog record has been requested for this book

ISBN: 978-0-367-71395-9 (hbk)
ISBN: 978-0-367-71403-1 (pbk)
ISBN: 978-1-003-15068-8 (ebk)

DOI: 10.4324/9781003150688

Typeset in Baskerville
by codeMantra

Contents

Contributor Bios

Asgeir Falch-Eriksen is a head of academic unit at the Department of Social Work, Child Welfare and Social Policy. He has a PhD in political science and specializes in political theory, legal philosophy and the sociology of the professions. He has published multiple research reports on Norwegian child protection and further publications on the interconnection between child protection and human rights.

Rafaela Lehtme is a doctoral researcher of social work at the School of Governance, Law and Society, Tallinn University. Her main research focus is on child's best interests and well-being in the context of family dissolution/shared parenting. Research interests also include child participation and family engagement in child protection system and she is actively engaging in different research projects related to these topics.

Cecilie Basberg Neumann is a professor in sociology at Oslo Metropolitan University. She is also a Gestalt therapist and her professional interests are in professional social work, gender, class, methodology and social theory.

Koidu Saia is a doctoral researcher of social work and research coordinator at the School of Governance, Law and Society, Tallinn University. Her research interests are related to interprofessional collaboration, young offenders' rehabilitation and community support in rural areas. Her practical professional experience has been associated with supporting children and families at risks as a social pedagogue and a social worker.

Ingrid Sindi is a social work lecturer at the School of Governance, Law and Society, Tallinn University. Her research focuses on the changing concept of child in Estonian residential care and her research is connected with human rights of removed children as vulnerable groups, based on ethnographic research in substitute homes.

Karmen Toros is a professor of social work at the School of Governance, Law and Society, Tallinn University. She is actively involved in social work education and training of child protection workers. Her research focuses on child welfare and protection, strengths-perspective and solution-focused approach in child protection practice and is particularly interested in child protection assessment of children in need.

Preface

This volume is the product of a concerted effort to elevate a human rights perspective into social work professionalism. This academic endeavour has been motivated by a series of publications unveiling that children are not listened to throughout their casework in child protection services. Although we can see throughout the last decades that children's participation has received a great deal of attention within policy and practise internationally, the inclusion of children in the practical work on street level has yet to occur. This is unfortunate as the child has a right that quite explicitly demands that they are to participate in any and all administrative proceedings that affect them, that is, Art. 12 of the United Nations Convention on the Rights of the Child. Hence, this book is a matter of contributing to rectifying a great shortcoming to professional practice in child protection services.

This book is the outcome of the project *Enhancing Child's Right for the Participation in Child Protection Assessment* funded by EEA and Norway Grants 2014–2021, implemented by two universities – Tallinn University in Estonia and Oslo Metropolitan University in Norway. The main aim of this project is to promote current and future child protective workers' access to knowledge, and the continued effort to professionalize the workforce and their duty to enforce the rights of the child.

Asgeir Falch-Eriksen & Karmen Toros
Oslo/Tallinn, December 2021

Iceland
Liechtenstein
Norway grants

1 Children's Right to Express Themselves in Child Protection Casework

Asgeir Falch-Eriksen and Karmen Toros

As professionals in child protection services (CPS) meet their clients, who are children and their families, they are authorised to reach decisions, advise, and guide them to reach specific predefined social goals. A child subjected to detrimental care of any kind must be alleviated from their current care context, either in their homes or be removed from parental care altogether, parents who lack the competence to care adequately must be empowered to do so, children who drop out of school due to the needs of the family must be assisted and so on. In doing so, the professionals' reasoning and argumentation are driven towards decision-making presumptively guided by esoteric knowledge belonging to the profession they represent, which predominantly is social work. Professional knowledge must combine the authorisation to perform professional practice delegated through legal regulation that set restrictions on what professionals can and cannot do and needs to guide their reasoning towards decision-making. Said differently, professional decision-making, their autonomy to tailor decisions, cannot breach the legal authorisation they depend on to conduct professional practice, i.e. practice according to the social goal the letter of the law is set to achieve.

Within modern liberal constitutional democracies, the United Nations Convention on the Rights of the Child (CRC) has gained gradual support during the last three decades since introduced in 1989. Regarding CPS practices, virtually all countries in the world ascribe to the basic rights norms of the CRC and are subsequently striving towards answering the needs of the child as a matter of right.[1] Although the practical limitations towards implementing and enforcing the CRC abounds, the formal dedication to children's rights, by, for instance, embedding the CRC in national legislation or constitutionalising rights of children, is widespread. With these political-normative efforts, the CRC has also become an integral part of shaping professional practices and what practices to develop and introduce across countries. Combining the CRC with CPS practices is a recent endeavour throughout CPS history and is still ongoing. Hence, there is a

DOI: 10.4324/9781003150688-1

continuous need to develop and understand how the child's rights become an integral part of professional practices within and throughout CPS. Opposite, practices that do not meet the rights of the child, and where professionals do not maintain their delegated authority to conduct professional practice according to rights, run contrary to the social goal the CPS is set to reach. Therefore, such practices must be altered or replaced by adequate knowledge-based practices and simultaneously uphold and maintain the child's rights. As any country that claims to enforce the child's rights as a social goal, we can argue that street-level professionalism guiding CPS practices must maintain a human rights ethos.

In CPS practices, the lives of children and families are very often unique or should be treated as unique. Whenever a child or a parent raises some type of rights claims, they also invoke their individual circumstances, their own identity, their social network, and professionals who must answer these claims must address each situation with each individual in its own right in a coherent and non-discriminatory manner from one case to the next. The task laid upon the social work profession, the dominant profession within CPS practices, is massive and calls for the development of knowledge-based practices that can help professionals reach the social goals the CPS aims to achieve. How can we understand the implications of the delegated authority to conduct public protection of children subjected to detrimental care? How can we understand this connection when the authorisation of CPS practices involves enforcing the child's rights? More particular, how can we understand the child's right to express itself in casework that affects them by the CPS?

The notion of protecting children from harm is an old one and has been embedded one way or the other across countries throughout modern history. The significance of this trivial backdrop is that public protection of children has been driven by different social goals with various normative imprints competing with human rights. Allowing CPS practices to conform to demands set by human rights involves most fundamentally that the CPS must secure the child's right to freedom from violence through practices that rest firmly within a normative approach to professional practices based on a human rights ethos.

Many competing normative approaches, or social goals, are still prevalent from one nation-state to the next. For instance, a social goal can be to have an instrumental approach, where CPS is a public institution set merely to solve nation-state problems and must do so effectively, and usually about calculating the investment cost of "producing" children that do not end up as "social problems." Another social goal can be to let child protection be guided by communitarian norms, namely, to protect children according to some conception of the good, a conception of social life deemed as moral and expected to constitute a part of each citizen's iden-tity. A third social goal, which is very widespread, is to conceive of CPS as a welfare state practice set to counter material marginalisation, which is something distinct from protection against detrimental care. Contrary to these social goals is a human rights ethos that approaches CPS through neither norms of effectiveness nor any one type of moral conviction or as an effort to combat poverty. There are many other social goals, but the main point is that human rights and the human rights ethos that drives rights-based practices caves as a guiding norm to other basic normative approaches to CPS, human rights lose their purpose.

This book will narrow down what rights-based professional practices entail by focusing on one specific article of the CRC, namely, Article 12 – the child's right to express their views freely in matters that affect them. By focusing on Art. 12, we will be able to discuss how CPS practices can be developed to uphold a human rights standard professionally:

Article 12

1 States Parties shall assure to the child who is capable of forming his or her own views the right to express those views freely in all matters affecting the child, the views of the child being given due weight in accordance with the age and maturity of the child.
2 For this purpose, the child shall, in particular, be provided the oppor-tunity to be heard in any judicial and administrative proceedings affecting the child, either directly, or through a representative or an appropriate body, in a manner consistent with the procedural rules of national law.

Important to Art. 12 and the CPS is how that right works when adminis-trative and judicial proceedings affect children, and where a "child shall *in particular* be provided the opportunity to be heard." CPS practices affect the child, or at least this is the aim of its casework. Hence, Art. 12 is a legal norm that is hard to ignore and should pervade CPS practices. Not allowing the child to participate in an informed manner, enabling the child to express itself adequately, and taking the time to listen to what the child says easily becomes a breach of their rights. Exceptions can be made, but those exceptions must be legitimised as rights-based, and therefore always maintain the human rights demand to be in the child's best interests (cf. CRC Art. 3.1).

The rights of a child subjected to detrimental care depend on profes-sional practitioners knowing how to enforce their rights. As Chapter 2 will illuminate, the research literature documents extensively, and across countries, how rights of children and Art.12 are implemented either with the child's voice not being heard or as a pro-forma/tokenistic approach to listening to the child throughout CPS practices. This book will move one step further and discuss and attempt to explain how professional practices within CPS must be able to justify how Art.12 is enforced no matter where that CPS practice is located in the course of CPS casework, whether it is at home, in foster care, in institutional settings, through administrative systems or following up on severe at-risk children. Art.12 calls for comprehensive enforcement of a child's rights through CPS practices. A child affected by any CPS practice must be provided *"the opportunity to be heard"* in any administrative- and judicial proceedings.

As it is a lack of any detailed research-based knowledge on how to enforce Art.12 *throughout* CPS practices, it becomes correspondingly hard to justify that the child has a *de facto* right to be heard, albeit the right is formally in place throughout legislation and policy. This book will attempt to remedy the lack of literature on professional rights-based practice about Art.12. The book will also seek to contribute to the ongoing research agenda, combining an interest in developing rights-based and knowledge-based professional practice in social work.

The Normative Bias to Professional Practices – The Case of Article 12 of the CRC

The most widely used and common-sense approach to this right is to refer to it as hearing (the voice) of the child, listening to the child, the child's right to participation, or something equivalent. This can easily bring in a narrow normative interpretation of what is formally stipulated by the right itself. It calls for a mere exercise of listening to what a child utters. A human rights approach goes further and more profound (Baraldi & Cockburn, 2018). A fundamental principle of human rights alludes to the child's dignity, namely, that it is a freedom of expressing their preferred views in all matters that affect them *because* it affects them. It is not the mere freedom of expression, which is covered in CRC Art. 13, but a matter of allowing children to express their views when administrative or judicial proceedings affect them, and not in a performative manner, by providing information to the child, speaking to the child to understand the child, and thereby understand better what the child expresses, or would like to express (Nylund, 2020). Connected to this is the respect a child deserves as a fellow human being, and by that, I mean the respect embedded in the system of human rights, and that a rights-based system calls for respect for any individual because of their personhood and the inviolable character of their individual integrity, and that they are rational beings worthy of respect.

Although the scholarly focus revolving around CRC Art. 12 is rich and contributions abound (Archard & Skivenes, 2009; Dingwall et al., 2014), there is a lack of research literature that critically discusses professional enforcement of Art. 12 on street level in a coherent and advanced manner, and that also seek to be instructive for professionals (Berrick et al., 2015; Falch-Eriksen & Backe-Hansen, 2018; Falch-Eriksen & Skivenes, 2019). As most countries in the world argue that they abide by and enforce the CRC, and thereby the CRC Art. 12, the significant lack of literature that bridges the demand for implementing Art. 12 on the one hand to professional CPS practice on the other, tells us that most countries need the knowledge to close this gap and to be able to live up to their promise of reaching the social goal of protection from detrimental care according to rights (Falch-Eriksen et al., 2021; Toros, 2017; Toros & Falch-Eriksen, 2020).

The right to freedom from violence is imperative to rights-based CPS practices. Still, each right constitutes the building blocks of that which in the sum establishes *the legal status* of the child's citizenship, i.e. the "status of a legal personhood that carries a set of legally specified rights" (Cohen, 1999). The CRC's rights shape the child's *citizenship* with a cosmopolitan imprint, and which every child carries equally from one country to the next (Earls, 2011; Sierra-Cedillo et al., 2019). Hence, the catalogue of rights and the complexity it creates call for a wide range of considerations while developing professional practices. The substantial content of such citizenship, provided that human rights of citizens are sought to be respected and enforced by the nation-state, constitutes a formal, political, and normative reality that public practices within each country bend towards (Baraldi & Cockburn, 2018; Falch-Eriksen, 2018). By having human rights to guide CPS practices, there are corresponding and fundamental normative biases that guide practices and ensure the development of practices on meeting the needs of a child who carries a right to protection.

Consequently, human rights can have massive implications for social work professionalism and CPS practices *if* the country performs according to its self-imposed duty to enforce rights. CPS is a public service with a responsibility to enforce rights. A child's right to be protected from violence thereby sets the child's rights on trial; the more efficient a country is to enforce the child's rights, the stronger we can argue the child's citizenship becomes.

Although the CRC has a global reach and has a cosmopolitan normative imprint, the commitment to enforce it is often reaffirmed across very different countries and very different governments within these countries (Berrick et al., 2015). As countries implement and seek to enforce the child's rights, a margin of appreciation opens for variations according to each country's capabilities. However, human rights cannot altogether lose their intention by having different meanings on the outset from one country to the next or be enforced in a manner that makes professional rights-based practice completely different from one country to the next (Sandberg, 2018). If the promise of enforcing human rights for children is to be redeemed in any country, and in a meaningful way, rights claims of children must be met by public officials as far as possible according to an equal meaning of rights, and also according to an equal sense of rationality guiding professional practice. Since the CPS does not carry the authority to revoke human rights held by children and parents, nor diminish them or otherwise curtail them, services must answer professionally and coherently whenever rights claims are raised.

CPS practices, and whatever shape an office of CPS takes, are more than other public services, set to answer when rights are infringed on.[2] Children have the right to live a life free from violence (cf. CRC Art. 9 and 19), and the child-clients of CPS are always suspected of living according to some version of a threat towards such a right (we could even put parental neglect and parental incompetence into this broad conception of violence). And so, developing professional practices in CPS become inseparable from enforcing the child's rights (Falch-Eriksen & Backe-Hansen, 2018).

In this book, we picked Art.12 for three reasons. *First*, it is a right that is imperative in qualifying decisions to be in the child's best interests (i.e. upholding the fundamental CRC-right – Art. 3.1), which is supposed to be a primary consideration in every decision. *Second*, and as will become clear in Chapter 2, we know that CPS across countries has widespread shortcomings in implementing and understanding how this right works throughout professional practice. A *third* and a bit general note is that CPS practices cannot abide by the rights of the child. It is not a choice of the CPS to enforce this article or not. CPS cannot intentionally or unintentionally revoke the child's human rights irrespective of the CPS. Therefore, it is CPS's entire fault if the child's rights are not enforced with regard to the operative protection of children.

Article 12 and the Human Rights Standard

The key to embedding Art. 12 into rights-based professional practices is to understand the components belonging to Art. 12 by reconstructing a rationale that can be used as the normative justification of human rights practices. Only by tracing human rights back to its building blocks can a coherent rationale be built to understand the broader application of Art. 12 (Habermas, 2010; Kant, 1887). Such a theoretical exercise will also need to convey how rights should be understood as belonging to a child compared to adults and whose moral psychology is not yet developed during childhood (Nussbaum, 2019). Instead of elaborating on a broad discussion of the legitimacy of human rights altogether, we will simply reconstruct the human rights standard from its origin within international human rights instruments. Hence, we will begin with the first sentence of Art. 1 of the Universal Declaration of Human Rights and how it states the explicit commitment to protect the dignity of each person: "All human beings are born free and equal in dignity and rights." Although we could argue that this is a core intuition guiding human rights and also a sound point of departure for explaining how a human rights standard can be developed and understood, an essential justification for choosing dignity as a point of departure is that it empirically figures as one of the most critical points of references in the justification of human rights across human rights instruments (Habermas, 2010; Haugli et al., 2019).

Using dignity as a lever implies that seeing each human being as born free and equal in dignity conveys a deep, substantial cosmopolitan conviction of individual worth pushing the human rights agenda, which unlocks the reflexivity between the need for rights protections to safeguard individual dignity. It also implies that any human right can be seen as deduced from such a core condition, namely, to counter any detriment that falls upon the individual person whenever that person's dignity is threatened (Habermas, 2010). It is also one of the reasons human rights, in total, should be connected as indivisible, as they emanate from the same core motivation to protect dignity. Using dignity as a lever, a human rights standard rooted in the protection of individual dignity becomes the point of departure for developing a system of human rights where rights are interconnected through a common normative predisposition to upholding a thin conception of a universal morality through the enforcement of rights to protect individual dignity.

To understand how the dignity of each person can become protected, we will, in this book, argue the human rights standard calls for two fundamental demands that have become integral to any nation-state claiming to enforce human rights within a grander scheme of the democratic rule of law and public street-level services. To safeguard the dignity of each person, each person must be allowed to choose how to live life for themselves. Hence, the *first* demand is that the nation-state constitutionally secures the rights of private individuals to act freely following what their dignity prescribes, thereby through a right to liberty and according to their own rational self-interest. Each individual's right to liberty is as broad as possible, provided that all individuals carry an equal amount of liberties (Dworkin, 1977). *Second*, individuals can agree to collective regulation through the rule of law since the legal order is constrained and guided by the constitutionality of human rights. Rights as constraints imply that legal development, policies, budgets, and public practices within public sectors will become reasonable as they do not infringe upon the liberties that rights already prescribe for each individual (Rothstein, 1998; Shapiro, 1999).

Combining these two demands, a legal order that regulates society, and in our case, the CPS becomes the product of the combination of constitutionally embedded rights and a legally regulated public service through self-government. The two demands can also be understood when viewing CRC Art. 12. Art. 12 is both a constitutionally embedded right of the individual child to freedom of expression, but it is also both a constitutional constraint and a guiding norm for how CPS practices are supposed to work. To enforce Art. 12 and let that particular right guide legal development, organisational designs, and professional practice, the child must be provided with the opportunity to express itself in all "judicial and administrative proceedings affecting the child." This implies almost any type of professional decision-making within the CPS.

Human Rights Standard, the Fiduciary Role of CPS, and the Child's Best Interests

How, then, does Art. 12 work as a constitutional right of the child, and as a restraint and a guiding norm for the professional practice of the CPS? What does it imply as a basic freedom for a child? Basic to fundamental constitutional rights are negative rights that constitute freedom from interference and are often referred to as liberty rights (cf. Berlin, 1958; Habermas, 1996). Not all constitutional rights are negative rights, but Art. 12, which provides a freedom to express views in casework that affects the child as a rights-holder, is such a liberty right. However, while individual freedom prescribed by rights depends on individuals' capacity to act rationally and according to socially acceptable norms, what Rawls refers to as two moral powers (Rawls, 1993), we cannot automatically provide a complete set of liberties to children. First, in general, children have not yet developed a coherent rational conception of how to live their lives, which implies knowing what to strive for and what the person wants. Second, children do not have sufficient insight, although it is gained gradually through maturity, of how to act in a manner that does not violate others acting upon their rights (Rawls, 1993).

The child's general lack of ability to act on their liberty rights is key to understanding the fiduciary role of parents and CPS practices. Until a child has the capacity to act freely, it will need other people's reasons to qualify decision-making to align with the child's best interests. As a child expresses itself, CPS professionals must remain vigilant in evaluating whether or not what is expressed is reasonable, how it can contribute to shape decision-making and to what degree it is in line with what can be claimed to be the child's best interests as part of the child's own rational plan of life, i.e. what is in line with that individual's self-interest. In most cases, the parents would carry this fiduciary role, but for children subjected to detrimental care, it would be the professionals within the CPS. In both cases, though, a child's right to act on their negative right to liberty becomes the fiduciary responsibility of adults.

Irrespective of the necessary fiduciary control and constraint on a child's expressions, which is called upon to reach decisions that align with the child's self-interest, a child carries a prospective right to individual freedom in the sense that a child receives access to a complete set of rights once it reaches adulthood (Falch-Eriksen, 2012). Until then, the child as a rights-holder remains a special case setting them apart from adults and making children dependent on a fiduciary principle that enables CPS professionals to carry the duty to interpret and understand the child's expressions and how it aligns with the child's best interests on its path towards adulthood. To underline how CPS professionals are obligated to approximate the child's self-interest and locate the child's developmental path from the point of view of securing the dignity of each person, we can look to CRC Art. 39: "States Parties shall take all appropriate measures to promote physical and psychological recovery and social reintegration of a child victim of any form of neglect, exploitation, or abuse…." What is implied is that professionals must ensure that the child's developmental trajectory is set on a path to recovery according to each particular child's best interest.

To qualify a decision in the best interests of the child, CPS professionals cannot merely listen to the child here and now or assume the information conveyed by the child's expressions is a separate issue altogether from CPS practices but must understand how the child's expressions align with the child's perspective right to liberty also in the long run, i.e. its future self-interests. The child's perspective right to individual liberty points into the distant future of the child – towards each particular child's adulthood and where the child becomes autonomous and receives rights as a full-fledged citizen.

Regulating CPS through Human Rights

In modern complex democracies, law-making assemblies regulate CPS primarily through legislative action and the delegation of authority. This holds true irrespective of what shape the organisation of the CPS takes from one country to the next. The delegation of authority is needed as CPS must have the possibility to intervene in the privacy of family life and perhaps remove the child coercively from the parents. As it thereby involves revoking fundamental rights of parents and children, this type of authorisation must be ensured to be in accordance with the law and legitimised from one case to the next. As such, the delegation of authority defines a formal jurisdiction for CPS professionals who work operatively on street level in face-to-face work with clients and demands of them to uphold the law and the rights of citizens throughout practices (Lipsky, 2010; Molander et al., 2012; Rothstein, 1998).

Within the authorisation, CPS is obligated to enforce rights claims raised by each child citizen. Hence, human rights not only set limitations to what regular law can prescribe caseworkers to do but in each case, a citizen's rights claim must be addressed from that particular citizens' point of view. In this way, the knowledge base of the professions occupying public services on street level enters into a symbiotic relationship with the democratic rule of law in that decisions must be tailored in such a fashion as to address the rights-claims of the citizen itself (Falch-Eriksen, 2018; Molander et al., 2012).

Human rights are often embedded on a constitutional level to be upheld according to their intent – namely, that they are fundamental and cannot be set aside by any majority. Carried by each CPS client, i.e. the child and parents, rights set up restrictions on professional practices. Hence, it is not enough for human rights to be formally embedded in legal codes but must also serve as operative restraints and guiding norms for professional practice and decision-making for CPS practices not to breach the constitutional character of human rights. Rights-based practices can, for instance, work both to prevent unlawful interventions into the private homes of families and set the threshold for when interventions must occur to protect a child from detrimental care. This also does not mean that constitutional rights must be formally embedded in regular law, but rather that stable principles of practice within CPS uphold the constitutional rights norms of human rights through professional practice and as part of a professional ethos.

Legal regulation becomes an integral part of CPS practices, and it does so in especially two separate ways. The *first* is the delegation of authority to practice and reach decisions in particular cases. The delegation stipulates that any CPS must not only uphold and enforce the rules of the delegation but must also enforce the meaning and intent of the delegated authority to not be in breach of the rule of law. For instance, whenever judicial and administrative proceedings affect a child, the CPS must act on the child's right to express itself or otherwise explain why it is in the child's best interests not to be listened to. Any administrative or judicial decision reached that does not listen to what the child expresses, or does not provide the reason for why this case calls for not listening, is in breach of such a rule. If it is going to work, rights-based practices become what Dworkin refers to as "standards set by a particular authority" (Dworkin, 1977).

The *second* is that the delegation of authority leaves a negative space for CPS professionals to fill, i.e. a decisional autonomy restrained by regulation. Regulation thereby opens up an area of autonomy for CPS that "does not exist except as an area left open by a surrounding belt of restrictions" (Dworkin, 1977). Decisional autonomy is a key trait for professional caseworkers, namely, the need to tailor decision-making to particular cases and where the tailoring itself upholds the normative intent of human rights norms. Hence, professional practitioners need to step in and perform judgment in each case.

Rights-Based Practice and Discretion

At the heart of professional practice stand decisional autonomy, also more commonly referred to as discretion (Abbott, 2014; Freidson, 2001; Molander, 2016). Although different definitions can be sought out, they generally share the notion of involving knowledge-based and knowledge-driven face-to-face decision-making undertaken by professionals (Goodin, 1986; Lipsky, 2010; Molander, 2016). In CPS casework, it is the process of deciding whether to protect a child or not, according to the child's specific care context and needs. In the process of doing so – every joint of a child's casework must heed the rights carried by the child as part of how professional practice is conducted. Professionals' decision-making must be completed in such a manner that they make a claim on correct and justified action, and where the warrants of action are shaped by the knowledge corpus of the profession itself (Molander et al., 2012).

To discretion, we can argue there are three basic components important to understand provided how professionals conduct practices according to the public mandate of the CPS (Molander, 2016). *First* is what we have already mentioned in the structure for decision-making, i.e. the restrictions created through regulation, and that defines an area of decisional autonomy bestowed on each professional CPS practitioner through a formal delegation of authority. Depending on the character of this delegation is the degree to which discretion is strong or weak, narrow or wide, formal or not (Goodin, 1986). *Second* is the process of care diagnostics, which is about evaluating the rights claim of the child through the CPS professionals fiduciary responsibility to understand that claim on the child's behalf, and to understand it as a matter of the child's context of care, the child's needs, and most importantly what is in the child's best interests (Falch-Eriksen, 2018). *Third*, it is the professional guiding norms that professionals must resort to while making decisions. This has to do with the continuous process of embedding rights-based practices, i.e. practices that uphold the child's rights epistemically through knowledge-based professional practice. From the point of view of professional practice, the delegation of discretionary powers down to social workers in CPS is based on the epistemic assumption that the professionals entrusted with the authority to act on discretion are those most capable of passing reasoned judgements to enforce rights. Currently, research suggests that they do not, but we are not making empirical claims here. If rights-based practices ought to work, we argue the case for rights-based professionalism. This implies professional practices being developed using a human rights standard as a primary design criterion.

The Progression of the Book

The book has seven chapters in addition to this introduction. The aim is to pass through significant parts of CPS practices where Art. 12 must be enforced. As the book treats CPS practices as dominated by administrative proceedings, there are no areas across CPS casework where the child is not set up for having the right to express itself. Even the word casework alludes to administrative proceedings and calls for the child to express itself. However, arguments can be made for children *not* to be allowed to express themselves due to age, maturity, drug- or alcohol abuse, anti-social behaviour, and so on, but the point of departure is that either children are going to express themselves or reasons must be provided that legitimises *not* listening to children from within a rights-based perspective.

In Chapter 2, Karmen Toros will lay out how Art. 12 of the CRC is one of the most complex and sensitive challenges to CPS practices. This chapter is a review of the academic literature, examining how Article 12 of the CRC is manifested in research and practice and where a missing link exists between professional practice in the CPS and Article 12. The presentation of the literature review will unveil that across countries children do not participate in CPS decision-making processes albeit the casework is aimed at the lives of the children and what is wrong with their care. Across the board, there are major shortcomings in that children are not listened to or heard and are practically invisible in the casework despite the ratification of the CRC, and that children carry rights.

In Chapter 3, Asgeir Falch-Eriksen seeks to lay out a manner in which to understand how professional practitioners can apply a human rights standard on to decision-making, ensuring that decisions do not breach the rights of the child. The human rights standard has its origin in the aim of human rights to secure dignity of each individual person. Using this insight in CPS practices and in combination with the child's right to express itself in administrative proceedings that affect their lives, it will be argued that listening to the child becomes imperative to understand how to safeguard and protect the dignity of the individual child. It is argued that

Art. 12 must be understood as a device that enables the child to assist and inform what is in the child's best interest, which is a primary consideration in rights-based practices according to CRC Art. 3.1.

In Chapter 4, Karmen Toros and Rafaela Eugenie Simonee Lehtme discuss how CPS conduct assessments, and how these assessments activate children's rights in a particular manner as the CPS must intervene based on the apparent risk to the child. Article 12 of the CRC dictates that certain components of the assessment must directly address children's rights. In their chapter, they discuss child protection assessments based on empirical data collected from registered children in need in CPS in Estonia, focusing on children's experiences during the assessment process. Children's perspectives are explained in the context of international studies to elaborate the role of Article 12 of the CRC across the field of practice.

In Chapter 5, Elisabeth Baasberg Neumann explores how CPS conduct follow-up of children who are placed outside the home. Central to the chapter is a study of how the child's right to express himself in his own case relates to the concept of relationship in the CPS follow-up of children placed in foster homes and emergency homes. The starting point for the discussions is that the CPS's obligation to enforce Article 12 of the CRC is indisputable and that the child is a bearer of rights. At the same time, the institutional framework for social workers' fulfilment of Article 12 is that this requirement meets a complex reality. In considering those complex realities, it is often difficult to see how social workers may realize the child's right, given existing institutional frameworks limited by time and task, and in particular as the fulfilment of rights connects intimately with the establishing of a secure relationship between the child and the social worker. In other words, children's rights to express themselves in their own case during follow-up in a foster home is a right that can easily be overlooked or put under pressure by caseworkers and supervisors in busy bureaucracies.

In Chapter 6, Koidu Saia discusses how CRC Art. 12 have implications for children who are placed in the juvenile justice system, where proceedings very often are either of an administrative or judicial character. The chapter explores participation particularly in cases with dually involved children, i.e., children that are involved in both the criminal justice system and the child protection system. This particular demographic constitutes one of the lead challenges for the CPS, as their involvement in casework is imperative to enforcing the rights of the child. The chapter focus on Article 12 and how rehabilitation works according to principles of proceedings pertaining to a broader scheme of a child-friendly justice system.

In Chapter 7, Ingrid Sindi focuses on children who have been placed in residential care (children living in substitute homes), and the obligations these cases create for professionals in CPS and among other caregivers, with reference to Article 12 of the CRC. Professionals within child protective services and direct caregivers have a particular responsibility for these children, as children in public care are therefore outside a normal family context while still having the same core human needs, such as the need to feel loved. Using examples from an ethnographic study in Estonia, the aim is to reflect on the concept of love through the disciplinary lens of new sociological research on childhood and children's rights, specifically, rights-based child residential care. In addition, citizenship is considered in this chapter to complement the discussion about children's autonomy, participation and need to feel loved and how this element can be placed within the context of rights-based child residential care.

Notes

1 The United States is an exception since it has not ratified the CRC. However, the opposition towards the CRC does not seem to be about CPS practices, and so the argument made here can also be relevant to the discourse on CPS practices in the U.S.
2 We will return in Chapter 3 to how children constitute a special case concerning raising rights claims.

Bibliography

Abbott, A. (2014). *The System of Professions: An Essay on the Division of Expert Labor.* Chicago, IL: University of Chicago Press.

Archard, D., & Skivenes, M. (2009). Hearing the child. *Child & Family Social Work, 14*(4), 391–399. doi:10.1111/j.1365-2206.2008.00606.x

Baraldi, C., & Cockburn, T. (2018). Introduction: Lived citizenship, rights and participation in contemporary Europe. In C. Baraldi & T. Cockburn (Eds.), *Theorising Childhood* (pp. 1–27). Cham: Springer International Publishing.

Berlin, I. (1958). *Two Concepts of Liberty. An Inaugural Lecture Delivered before the University of Oxford on 31 October 1958.* Oxford: Clarendon.

Berrick, J.D., Peckover, S., Poso, T., & Skivenes, M. (2015). The formalized framework for decision-making in child protection care orders: A cross-country analysis. *Journal of European Social Policy, 25*(4), 366–378. doi:10.1177/0958928715594540

Cohen, J.L. (1999). Changing paradigms of citizenship and the exclusiveness of the demos. *International Sociology, 14*(3), 245–268. doi:10.1177/0268580999014003002

Dingwall, R., Eekelaar, J., & Murray, T. (2014). *The Protection of Children: State Intervention and Family Life* (Vol. 16). New Orleans, LA: Quid Pro Books.

Dworkin, R. (1977). *Taking Rights Seriously* (New impression with a reply to critics. ed.). London: Duckworth.

Earls, F. (2011). Children: From rights to citizenship. *The Annals of the American Academy of Political and Social Science, 633*(1), 6–16. doi:10.1177/0002716210383637

Falch-Eriksen, A. (2012). The promise of trust – An inquiry into the legal design of coercive decision-making in Norway. In: HiOA Avhandling: 2012/5, https://hdl.handle.net/10642/1355

Falch-Eriksen, A. (2018). Rights and professional practice: How to understand their interconnection. In *Human Rights in Child Protection* (pp. 39–58). Cham: Palgrave Macmillan.

Falch-Eriksen, A., & Backe-Hansen, E. (2018). Child protection and human rights: a call for professional practice and policy. In A. Falch-Eriksen & E. Backe-Hansen (Eds.), *Human Rights in Child Protection*. London: Palgrave Macmillan. https://doi.org/10.1007/978-3-319-94800-3_1

Falch-Eriksen, A., & Skivenes, M. (2019). 3. Right to protection. In M. Langford, M. Skivenes, & K. H. Søvig (Eds.), *Children's Rights in Norway: An Implementation Paradox?* (pp. 107–135). Universitetsforlaget. https://doi.org/10.18261/9788215031415-2019-04 ER

Falch-Eriksen, A., Toros, K., Sindi, I., & Lehtme, R. (2021). Children expressing their views in child protection casework: Current research and their rights going forward. *Child & Family Social Work, n/a*(n/a). doi: 10.1111/cfs.12831

Freidson, E. (2001). *Professionalism: The Third Logic*. Cambridge: Polity Press.

Goodin, R.E. (1986). Welfare, rights and discretion. *Oxford Journal of Legal Studies, 6*(2), 232–261. doi:10.1093/ojls/6.2.232

Habermas, J. (1996). *Between Facts and Norms.Contributions to a Discourse Theory of Law and Democracy* (W. Rehg, Trans.). Cambridge, MA: The MIT Press.

Habermas, J. (2010). The concept of human dignity and the realistic utopia of human rights. *Metaphilosophy, 41*(4), 464–480. doi: 10.1111/j.1467-9973.2010.01648.x

Haugli, T., Nylund, A., Sigurdsen, R., & Bendiksen, L.R. (2019). *Children's Constitutional Rights in the Nordic Countries*. Leiden: Brill.

Kant, I. (1887). *The Philosophy of Law: An Exposition of the Fundamental Principles of Jurisprudence as the Science of Right*. Clark, NJ: Lawbook Exchange.

Lipsky, M. (2010). *Street-Level Bureaucracy: Dilemmas of the Individual in Public Service*. New York: Russell Sage Foundation.

Molander, A. (2016). *Discretion in the Welfare State: Social Rights and Professional Judgment* (Vol. 129). Abingdon, Oxon: Routledge.

Molander, A., Grimen, H., & Eriksen, E.O. (2012). Professional discretion and accountability in the welfare state. *Journal of Applied Philosophy, 29*(3), 214–230. doi:10.1111/j.1468-5930.2012.00564.x

Nussbaum, M.C. (2019). *The Cosmopolitan Tradition*. Cambridge, MA: Harvard University Press.

Nylund, A. (2020). Children's right to participate in decision-making in Norway: Paternalism and autonomy. In T., Haugli, A. Nylund, R. Sigurdsen and L.R.L. Bendiksen (Eds.), (pp. 201–224). Leiden: Brill Nijhoff.

Rawls, J. (1993). *Political Liberalism*. New York: Columbia University Press.

Rothstein, B. (1998). *Just Institutions Matter. The Moral and Political Logic of the Universal Welfare State*. Cambridge: Cambridge University Press.

Sandberg, K. (2018). Children's right to protection under the CRC. In A. Falch-Eriksen and E. Backe-Hansen (Eds.), *Human Rights in Child Protection* (pp. 15–38). London: Palgrave Macmillan.

Shapiro, I. (1999). *Democratic Justice*. New Haven, CT: Yale University Press.

Sierra-Cedillo, A., Sánchez, C., Figueroa-Olea, M., Izazola-Ezquerro, S., & Rivera-González, R. (2019). Children's participative citizenship within the context of integral care and daily life. *Early Child Development and Care, 189*(6), 883–895. doi:10.1080/03004430.2017.1345897

Toros, K. (2017). Child protective workers' reflections on principles underpinning the assessment of children in need: The case of Estonia. *International Social Work, 60*(5), 1255–1267. doi:10.1177/0020872815620261

Toros, K., & Falch-Eriksen, A. (2020). "I do not want to cause additional pain …"–child protection workers' perspectives on child participation in child protection practice. *Journal of Family Social Work*, 1–17. doi:10.1080/10522158.2020.1833396

2 Rights-Based Professional Practice

Situating the Academic Discourse

Karmen Toros

The Convention on the Rights of the Child (CRC, 1989) grants children the right to participate in matters affecting their lives and is considered to be a primary guiding instrument for practitioners to use in their decision-making (Kennan et al., 2018). Child welfare professionals have the lead role in encouraging vulnerable children to participate in child protection proceedings where decisions are made about their futures, including separation and removal from their families. These are complex and difficult decisions (Isokuortti et al., 2020; Russ et al., 2020) that have an enormous impact on the lives of children and families (Benbenishty et al., 2015). Therefore, this process requires the active involvement of the children themselves, indicating the need for rights-based professional development in child protective services (CPS) in order to enhance participatory practice and enable all children to have access to effective participation (Falch-Eriksen et al., 2021).

Children's participation in decisions affecting their lives is a fundamental human right (Brunnberg & Visser-Schuurman, 2015). Collins (2017) emphasises that even though child participation is advocated for as a fundamental human right, implementation remains challenging in practice. Seim and Slettebø (2017, p. 882) express similar thoughts regarding participatory practice as 'messier and more complicated than the policy rhetoric suggests'. Even though, according to international conventions, children are seen as subjects with rights of their own (Duncan, 2019), in practice children are still passive bystanders. This assertion is by no means new, but rather a reflection of an old and continuing problem. This is also confirmed by consistent findings of children not participating, not being listened to, and not being heard in CPS practice throughout the last decade in different countries (Falch-Eriksen et al., 2021; Toros, 2021a, 2021b).

Enabling children to have a voice about matters that directly affect their lives is not only a question of their rights, but is consistent with the values of the social work profession (Strolin-Goltzman et al., 2010). De Mönnink

DOI: 10.4324/9781003150688-2

(2017) considers human rights to be the motivation and justification for social work action. Schmidt et al. (2020) refer to the International Federation of Social Workers recognition of social work as a human rights profession that can promote the rights of oppressed groups. In general, I would not use the term 'oppressed' for children, but in the context of participatory practices in CPS, I argue that children are left in this position by adults – social workers, child protective workers, and other professionals working with children in need. There are various reasons for the lack of engagement between children and CPS which will be addressed later in this chapter, however, I first want to underline the importance of every child having the right to meaningful participation.

Based on Article 12 of the CRC, CPS practice is not in accordance with the convention if workers do not seek to understand the desires and needs of the children they are servicing, regardless of the child's age or capability. This article establishes that this right is not only fundamental but that it should also be considered in the interpretation and implementation of all other rights (see GC No. 12). Duramy and Gal (2020) recognise Article 12 rightfully as the CRC's innovative contribution to children's rights discourse. van Bijleveld et al. (2015) argue that children ought to participate in matters concerning them right from the start. They elaborated this thought further by noting, 'as long as social workers start the participation process after they have made the first decisions, children will not be able to participate in the way they want or in a way that recognises their human rights' (p. 137). Therefore, promoting rights-based professionalisation of CPS practices means that nation-states claiming to enforce the CRC must design CPS practices in such a way that children can express their views and have these views heard whenever they are relevant (Falch-Eriksen et al., 2021). A further requirement needed for rights-based CPS casework is for the primary consideration in decision-making to always be the best interests of the individual child (cf. CRC, Art. 3.1).

Decisions in the Best Interests of the Child

In order to discuss children's best interests, I want to outline an essential statement made by Skivenes (2020) – 'only the individual her/himself can determine what makes her/him happy and feeling well'. Here the right to participation becomes imperative to learn what is in the child's best interest. She elaborates an important notion that children do not determine their best interest, but require engagement in this process. In other words, the best interests of the child are established together with the child (GC No. 12).

I strongly agree with the argument that only the individual knows their own needs and wishes. As the best interests principle is every child's right, it 'must form part of the legal decision-making relating to their care and protection' (Walsh, 2020, p. 223). Furthermore, McCafferty (2022, p. 439) emphasises the ethical principles at the core of this profession by citing Bartoli and Dolan (2014), who explain that in decision-making processes 'child welfare professionals are entrusted both ethically and legally with acting in children's best interests and deciding where and how those best interests are met'. The rationale is that children can provide significant information and insight into their perspectives and experiences, which enables adults to make more informed decisions, leading to more effective interventions and outcomes (Johnson & West, 2018). Pećnik et al. (2016) outline here a crucial remark – involving the child in the decision-making process leads to better decisions because children's opinions and ideas are based on perceptions and experiences that differ from those of adults.

Aadnanes and Gulbrandsen (2017, p. 595) elaborate that children's definitions and understandings of their situations and their subsequent coping strategies are important knowledge for child welfare professionals to incorporate into their assessments and interventions. All children and their families are unique, including their needs and resources, making it necessary to acknowledge the importance of listening to their stories, constructing solutions, and making decisions in the best interests of the child. Learning from children's experiences is essential to better understand their needs (Bouma et al., 2018; Schoch et al., 2020). In addition, the process of understanding, motivating, and working towards desired outcomes differs among families and depends on various circumstances (Monclús et al., 2021), which again underscores the importance of children's participation in child protection proceedings and of regarding them as cognizant social actors (Schoch et al., 2020). As GC No. 12 stipulates, simply hearing what a child says is insufficient. Practitioners must actively listen to children express their hopes and fears, and seriously consider their **voices** when the child is capable of forming their own views (p. 18). Pećnik et al. (2016, p. 401) emphasise the phrase 'taken seriously' – 'the right to have the child's opinion heard and taken seriously applies to all actions and decisions that affect the lives of children'. Involving children in the decision-making process involves ensuring their voice is directly or indirectly represented (Muench et al., 2017). We need to remember or remind ourselves that children are the experts in their own lives (Toros et al., 2013; Toros & LaSala, 2019). Therefore, children's experiences cannot be understood without asking them directly, as they are the ones who can guide others to learn about their lives, what is in their interest and what they want (Bessant & Broadley, 2014).

Furthermore, studies emphasise the importance of participation for children's development, especially for children in care (O'Hare et al., 2016; Seim & Slettebø, 2017). In addition to participation being a positive influence on care outcomes, it also enhances children's understanding and trust in decision-making procedures (Bouma et al., 2018; Pećnik et al., 2016) and contributes to the development of informed decision-making (Alfandari, 2017; Berrick et al., 2015). These are all contributing factors in determining the best interests of the child, therefore, the decision-making process requires the child's opinions and preferences to be listened to and taken seriously. Article 12, in outlining the principle of child participation, is viewed as a cornerstone of the CRC in practicing rights-based child protection work (Bennouna et al., 2017; Rap et al., 2019; Tisdall, 2016). Article 12 thereby plays an integral role in ensuring that decisions can claim to be in the child's best interests. It should be emphasised that children's participation as well as their best interests are not only relevant for case-specific decisions, but also for creating the system itself. Furthermore, practitioners must ensure that this participation is fundamentally meaningful in nature.

Meaningful Participation of Children and Participation Models

Björnsdóttir and Einarsdóttir (2017, p. 290) refer to Lansdown (2010), who claimed that there is no explicit definition of the concept of child participation, which seems to be a rather broad (Seim & Slettebö, 2017) and a complex idea with multiple interpretations not strictly adhering to a single explanation (Herbots & Put, 2015). According to Wenger (1998, p. 56), complexity lies in combining different components such as doing, talking, thinking, feeling, and belonging (cf. Clement & McKenny, 2019). van Bijleveld et al. (2014) define participation as a situational and iterative process in which all relevant actors enter into mutual dialogue. Pölkki et al. (2012) similarly use the term 'interaction' to describe participation. Partridge (2005, p. 181) connects participation to dialogue as well, describing it as a 'two-way active involvement' in decision-making. Others also relate participation to the ability to influence or be part of making decisions (Duramy & Gal, 2020; Kriz & Roundtree-Swain, 2017). For example, Lundy (2007) discusses participation in terms of fostering dialogue between different stakeholders and influencing decision-making. Hart (1992) refers to participation as the process of sharing decisions that affect a child's life. Bolin's (2018) perspective on participation captures both of these viewpoints, describing it as 'bidirectional influences'. GC No. 12 describes participation as an 'ongoing process, which includes information-sharing and dialogue between children and adults based on mutual respect, and in which children can learn how their views and those of adults are taken into account and shape the outcome of such processes' (p. 5). This approach acknowledges the child as the expert of their own life (Husby et al., 2018). To conclude, participation is a multidimensional process (Gordon, 2015), which scholars generally associate with concepts like 'interaction/dialogue' and 'influence' and is recurrent by nature, not a single event.

As I outlined, participation cannot be seen as a simple and straightforward act. Invitation to participation does not automatically indicate that a child's views will be listened to (Collins, 2017). It is not enough only to include a child passively for tokenistic, ticking-the-box reasons. Inchaurrondo et al. (2018) also believe that child participation must be active participation, which incorporates the possibility of expressing opinions, needs, and fears. Access to information is another important element of meaningful participation (Middel et al., 2021). These factors combined create true, meaningful, and inclusive practice (Collins et al., 2021), involving the child from the starting point of an intense exchange between children and adults (GC No. 12, p. 7).

Bouma et al. (2018) use the term meaningful participation with reference to Pölkki et al. (2012, p. 109) who explain it as such: 'before being able to participate in administrative proceedings, children need information about contexts and procedures to decide if they find the situation safe, meaningful, or otherwise worth participating in'. Furthermore, Bouma et al. (2017) constructed a model of meaningful child participation in the child protection system based on empirical studies and theoretical child participation models from Hart (1992), Shier (2001), and the CRC Article 12. This model consists of three main dimensions: informing, hearing, and involving. Informing includes possibilities to participate, knowing the aim of participation, content, decisions, etc.; hearing incorporates possibilities to express views and opinions, gathering information from the child, dialogue with the child, and individual meetings with the child; and involving consists of hearing opinions and views before decisions are made, inclusion in decision-making and considering the child's perspectives (cf. Lauri et al., 2021, p. 213).

Some other scholars have developed similar standards for child participation. For example, Franklin and Sloper (2005) discuss children's participation within the framework of the CRC in terms of three participation levels – being informed, expressing views, and influencing decisions – to become a 'main decider'. Lundy (2007) developed a four-interrelated-element model in relation to CRC Article 12, consisting of space (opportunity to express views), voice (facilitation to voice views), audience (listening), and influence (decisions based on the voice). These three models are in basic agreement with each other – for participation to take place, interaction and dialogue with the child are required. This strengthens the concept of participation as an active process, not simply asking questions but active involvement in decision-making and a dialogue between the child and the protection worker based on the CRC Article 12.2 (cf. Toros, 2021a, p. 397). Meaningful participation strengthens children's trust in adults and in child welfare workers (Duramy & Gal, 2020), which in turn enables them to act in the best interest of children and increase their well-being and quality of services. Meaningful participation also aligns with the 3 Ps of the CRC, discussed in the previous sub-chapter. Despite existing models, achieving meaningful participation is challenging to implement in practice. This reality raises an important question: why is CPS practice not based on children's right to participate in decisions concerning their well-being and lives?

Children's Participation in the Decision-Making Process

Making decisions that affect the lives of children is a complicated responsibility (Duncan, 2019; Stokes & Schmidt, 2012), as these decisions often involve limited knowledge, some degree of uncertainty, time constrains, and powerful emotions (De Haan et al., 2019; Whittaker, 2018). Sandberg (2018, p. 31), referring to the CRC, emphasises that in order to reach decisions that are in the best interests of a child, 'in any decision-making, it is a child's right to express views and have them taken into account'. Even though research indicates that children are not able to participate in decision-making processes often enough and their voices are either not being heard or not taken seriously (Husby et al., 2018; Kosher & Ben-Arieh, 2020; van Bijleveld et al., 2020), professionals generally agree that effective decisions require the participation of children. Therefore, the question remains – we agree that children should participate, yet we fail to listen their voices and do not include them in decision-making processes – why? Staudt et al. (2012) discuss multiple layers of influence that affect the realities and complexities of participatory practices.

Lack of child participation in decision-making is influenced by a number of organisational constraints, such as time and workload (Husby et al., 2018). Bastian (2019) points out that a high workload erodes professional judgement, which may result in a failure to appreciate the importance of children's voices. According to Lundy (2018), time constraints result in tokenistic participation. Other scholars emphasise children being unheard in CPS due to managerialism (Bolin, 2018; Munro & Turnell, 2018; Rogowski, 2020). As discussed by Munro (2010), managerialism has contributed to creating a very controlled and proceduralised workforce that mitigates learning and adapting in response to new information. As a result, decision-making concerning children's welfare leads to a 'procedure-driven, child-unfriendly environment' (van Bijleveld et al., 2015). It is essential to remember that children are the centre of child protection work and not bureaucracy. Burton and Revell (2018) argue that managerialism hinders seeing, feeling, and experiencing child protection interventions. On this note, Bolin (2018) believes that children's participation needs to be recognised morally, as a resource for promoting service efficacy that is supported by organisational values focusing on client-worker relationships.

Benson and Rosen (2017) argue that the protectionist approach is a possible explanation for the absence of children's voices in child protection practice, their claim being supported by numerous studies (Kosher & Ben-Arieh, 2020; van Bijleveld et al., 2020). This approach could be an obstacle if professionals seek to protect children from harmful memories or uncomfortable discussions. Protectionism is linked to the idea of childhood being a time of innocence and vulnerability (Pinkey, 2018), leading practitioners to exclude children from child protection processes and decision-making to avoid potentially causing harm to the child. However, this only increases children's powerlessness to influence decisions about their lives (Fern, 2014), therefore working against the rights of the child.

Muench et al. (2017) state that children play a fundamental role in the planning and delivery of services. Participation here is viewed as a way of securing information or evidence that facilitates the making of a decision and its subsequent implementation (Archard & Skivenes, 2009). Some scholars use the term nexus – participation as a nexus of decision-making (Schoch et al., 2020). MacDonald (2017, p. 3) argues that 'children's perspectives should be included and considered not just because it is their right to be heard, but also because there is inherent value in the contributions children make to assessment and decision-making'. Enhancing children's participation is believed to improve society in general, as Hart (1992) pointed out decades ago. Björnsdóttir and Einarsdóttir (2017) discuss similar thoughts – participation can benefit both children and the society, whereas research refers to various negative effects on children in case of the lack of participation, such as children feeling worried, helpless, and angry (Husby et al., 2018).

Professionalism in Children's Participation in Child Welfare Practices

As child welfare professionals ensure children's safety (Olszowya et al., 2020), it is necessary to pose the question, 'What does it mean to be a child welfare professional?' Hart (1992, p. 32) outlined decades ago that 'the ability to truly participate depends on a basic competence in taking the perspective of other persons'. I again want to bring focus to the idea that the fulfilment of children's participatory rights depends upon professional practice and practitioners knowing how to enforce them. Bingle and Middleton (2019) agree that 'the context of child protection influences the worker's need for the right answer'. Similarly, it can be also said that the context serves as a restriction in the pursuit of the 'right answer', by which I mean the 'child's truth' – experiences, needs, hopes, etc.

It is easier to decide what is in the best interest of the child from the adult point of view, as we feel we always know what is good for children. Skivenes (2020) argues that reasons for this are 'the decision makers' adultism' and 'lack of a child-equality perspective'. Similarly, some other scholars consider the continuing support of a paternalistic ideology one of the reasons for ignoring children's right to participate (Collins, 2017; Duncan, 2019; Strömpl & Luhamaa, 2020). Kiraly and Humphreys (2013) argued almost a decade ago that adult perspectives continue to dominate and take priority over the wishes and needs of children, and we see the same trend in social work practice today. I firmly believe that adults cannot know the experience of children, even if they claim to. Saar-Heiman and Gupta (2020, p. 1168) state that the 'current neoliberal era has created a punitive, individualised, and pathologising child protection system', which weakens the child-centred paradigm of learning from children by seeing them as experts on their own lives.

Going further, I question whether children are not encouraged to participate because child welfare professionals do not understand the concept of child participation. Even though the concept is considered to be complex and multidimensional, as explained in the previous sub-chapter, it clearly emphasises children's active participation and the need for the child to be a part of the dialogue. Nevertheless, Kosher and Ben-Arieh (2020) argue that limited implementation of children's participation may indicate that professionals do not fully understand or appreciate the meaning and value of children's participation. Furthermore, various studies suggest that child welfare professionals lack the skills needed to communicate with children (Toros, 2021a; Toros & Falch-Eriksen, 2021), resulting in their exclusion from CPS work. Arbeiter and Toros (2017) suggest child protection workers lack the confidence to engage with children in decision-making processes due to insufficient skills and training, including building rapport and trusting relationships.

Bolin (2018) offers relation-oriented practical recommendations for strengthening child-centred practice, which she refers to as 'organizing children's agency' – accessibility of support services and innovative solutions for creating spaces for therapeutic talking with children. Gouldsboro (2018) explores how to listen to children's voices in practice based on the relational approach, comprising of several factors: being a positive role model, partnering with parents, understanding the stages of child development, giving children time, complete listening, and building quality interactions. I would argue that while the notion of a child as an active agent is no longer a new concept, child participation demands new way of thinking as the current system is not working for the children – it is time to put words into actions. I want to finish this chapter by stating that professionalism is more than just knowing what is right, but above all means doing what is right.

Acknowledgement

This chapter is informed by the 'Effective Participatory Discourse: Experiences of Participants' Engagement in the Context of Child Protection Assessment Practices' project, supported by the Estonian Research Council, grant number PSG305.

References

Aadnanes, M., & Gulbrandsen, L.M. (2017). Young people and young adults' experiences with child abuse and maltreatment: Meaning making, conceptualizations, and dealing with violence. *Qualitative Social Work*, *17*(4), 594–610.

Alfandari, R. (2017). Evaluation of a national reform in the Israeli child protection practice designed to improve children's participation in decision-making. *Child & Family Social Work*, *22*, 54–62.

Arbeiter, E., &Toros, K. (2017). Participatory discourse: Engagement in the context of child protection assessment practices from the perspectives of child protection workers, parents and children. *Children and Youth Services Review*, *74*, 17–27.

Archard, D., & Skivenes, M. (2009). Hearing the child. *Child and Family Social Work*, *14*, 391–399.

Bastian, C. (2019). The child in child protection: Invisible and unheard. *Child & Family Social Work*, *25*, 135–143.

Benbenishty, R., Davidson-Arad, B., López, M., Devaney, J., Spratt, T., Koopmans, C., Knorth, E.J., Witteman, C.l.M., Del Valle, J.F., & Hayes, D. (2015). Decision making in child protection: An international comparative study on maltreatment substantiation, risk assessment and interventions recommendations, and the role of professionals' child welfare attitudes. *Child Abuse & Neglect*, *49*, 63–75.

Bennouna, C., Mansourian, H., & Stark, L. (2017). Ethical considerations for children's participation in data collection activities during humanitarian emergencies: A Delphi review. *Conflict and Health*, *11*(5), 1–15.

Benson, L., & Rosen, R. (2017). From silence to solidarity: Locating the absent 'child voice' in the struggle against benefit sanctions. *Children & Society*, *31*, 302–314.

Berrick, J.D., Dickens, J., Pösö, T., & Skivenes, M. (2015). Children's involvement in care order decision-making: A cross-country analysis. *Child Abuse & Neglect*, *49*, 128–141.

Bessant, J., & Broadley, K. (2014). Saying and doing child protective service and participation in decision-making. *International Journal of Children's Rights*, *22*, 710–729.

van Bijleveld, G.G., Bunders-Aelen, J.F.G., & Dedding, C.W.M. (2020). Exploring the essence of enabling child participation within child protection services. *Child & Family Social Work*, *25*(2), 286–293.

van Bijleveld, G.G., Dedding, C.W.M., & Bunders-Aelen, J.F.G. (2014). Seeing eye to eye or not? Young people's and child protection workers' perspectives on children's participation within the Dutch child protection and welfare services. *Children and Youth Services Review*, *47*, 253–259.

van Bijleveld, G.G., Dedding, C.W.M., Bunders-Aelen, J.F.G. (2015). Children's and young people's participation within child welfare and child protection services: A state-of-the-art review. *Child & Family Social Work*, *20*, 129–138.

Bingle, L., & Middleton, A. (2019). From doing to being: The tensions of systemic practice in social work – group reflective supervision in child protection. *Journal of Family Therapy*, *41*, 384–406.

Björnsdóttir, Þ., & Einarsdóttir, J. (2017). Child participation in Ghana: Responsibilities and rights. In E. Oinas, H. Onodera, & L. Suurpää, L. (Eds.), *What Politics? Youth and Political Engagement in Africa* (pp. 285–299). Leiden, Boston, MA: Brill.

Bolin, A. (2018). Organizing for agency: Rethinking the conditions for children's participation in service provision. *International Journal of Qualitative Studies on Health and Well-Being*, *13*, 1564515.

Bouma, H., Knorth, E.J., Grietens, H., & López, M. (2017). *Betekenisvolle participatie van kinderen in de jeugdbescherming: Inzicht in het concept en de verankering in het Nederlandse jeugdbeschermingsbeleid*. Groningen: Rijksuniversiteit Groningen.

Bouma, H., López López, M., Knorth, E.J., & Grietens, H. (2018). Meaningful participation for children in the Dutch child protection system: A critical analysis of relevant provisions in policy documents. *Child Abuse & Neglect*, *79*, 279–292.

Brunnberg, E., & Visser-Schuurman, M. (2015). Speak up! Voices of European children in vulnerable situations. *International Journal of Children's Rights*, *23*, 569–601.

Burton, V., & Revell, L. (2018). Professional curiosity in child protection: Thinking the unthinkable in a neo-liberal world. *British Journal of Social Work*, *48*, 1508–1523.

Clement, M., & McKenny, R. (2019). Developing an Open Dialogue inspired model of systemic social work assessment in a local authority children's social care department. *Journal of Family Therapy*, *41*, 421–446.

Collins, T.M. (2017). A child's right to participate: Implications for international child protection. *The International Journal of Human Rights*, *21*(1), 14–46.

Collins, T.M., Sinclair, L.D., & Zufelt, V.E. (2021). Children's rights to participation and protection: Examining Child and Youth Care College Curricula in Ontario. *Child & Youth Services*, *42*(3), 268–297.

CRC (United Nations Convention on the Rights of the Child). (1989). New York: United Nations.

Duncan, M. (2019). Children's experiences of statutory child protection interventions. In M. Duncan (Ed.), *Participation in Child Protection. Theorizing Children's Perspectives* (pp. 13–42). Cham: Springer Nature Switzerland AG.

Duramy, B.F., & Gal, T. (2020). Understanding and implementing child participation: Lessons from the Global South. *Children and Youth Services Review, 119*, 105645.

Falch-Eriksen, A., Toros, K., Sindi, I., & Lehtme, R. (2021). Children expressing their views in child protection casework: Current research and their rights going forward. *Child & Family Social Work, 26*(3), 485–497.

Fern, E. (2014). Child-directed social work practice: Findings from an action research study conducted in Iceland. *British Journal of Social Work, 44*, 1110–1128.

Franklin, A., & Sloper, P. (2009). Supporting the participation of disabled children and young people in decision-making. *Children & Society, 23*(1), 3–15.

GC (General Comment) No. 12. (2009). *Convention on the Rights of the Child. The Right of the Child to be Heard.* United Nations. CRC/C/GC/12.

Gordon, L.N. (2015). Child participation in Jamaica: Cultural reality versus idealism. *Social and Economic Studies, Special Issue on Children – Reflections on adherence to Child Rights in the Caribbean, 64*(1), 49–74.

Gouldsboro, J.M. (2018). *The Voice of the Child. How to Listen Effectively to Young Children.* New York: Routledge.

De Haan, W.D., van Berkel, S.R., & van der Asdnok, S. (2019). Out-of-home placement decisions: How individual characteristics of professionals are reflected in deciding about child protection cases. *Developmental Child Welfare, 1*(4), 312–326.

Hart, R.A. (1992). *Children's Participation: From Tokenism to Citizenship.* Innocenti Essays, 4. Florence: UNICEF International Child Development Centre. https://www.unicef-irc.org/publications/pdf/childrens_participation.pdf

Herbots, K., & Put, J. (2015). The participation disc: A concept analysis of (a) child ('s right to) participation. *International Journal of Children's Rights, 23*(1), 154–188.

Husby, I.S.D., Slettebø, T., & Juul, R. (2018). Partnership with children in child welfare: The importance of trust and pedagogical support. *Child & Family Social Work, 23*, 443–450.

Inchaurrondo, A.M., Fuentes-Peláez, N., Vicente, C.P., & Bolós, A.M. (2018). Good professional practices for promoting positive parenting and child participation in reunification processes. *Child & Family Social Work, 23*, 574–581.

Isokuortti, N., Aaltio, E., Laajasalo, T., & Barlow, J. (2020). Effectiveness of child protection practice models: A systematic review. *Child Abuse & Neglect, 108*, 104632.

Johnson, V., & West, A. (2018). Introduction: Following the journey of voice In. V. Johnson & A. West (Eds.), *Children's Participation in Global Contexts: Going beyond the Voice* (pp. 3–13). New York: Routledge.

Kennan, D., Brady, B., & Forkan, C. (2019). Space, voice, audience and influence: The Lundy model of participation. *Child Welfare Practice, 31*(3), 205–218.

Kiraly. M., & Humphreys, C. (2013). Perspectives from young people about family contact in kinship care: "Don't push us listen more". *Australian Social Work, 66,* 314–327.

Kosher, H., & Ben-Arieh, A. (2020). Social workers' perceptions of children's right to participation. *Child & Family Social Work, 25*(2), 294–303.

Kriz, K., & Roundtree-Swain, D. (2017). "We are merchandise on a conveyer belt": How young adults in the public child protection system perceive their participation in decisions about their care. *Children and Youth Services Review, 78,* 32–40.

Lauri, K., Toros, K., & Lehtme, R. (2021). Participation in the child protection assessment: Voices from children in Estonia. *Child and Adolescent Social Work Journal, 38,* 211–226.

Lundy, L. (2007). 'Voice' is not enough: Conceptualizing Article 12 of the United Nations Convention on the Rights of the Child. *British Educational Research Journal, 33*(6), 927–942.

Lundy, L. (2018). In defence of tokenism? Implementing children's right to participate in collective decision-making. *Childhood, 25,* 340–354.

MacDonald, G.S. (2017). Hearing children's voices? Including children's perspectives on their experiences of domestic violence in welfare reports prepared for the English courts in private family law proceedings. *Child Abuse & Neglect, 65,* 1–13.

McCafferty, P. (2022). "Do I read it? No". Knowledge utilisation in child welfare decisions. *Child Care in Practice, 28*(3), 438–463.

Middel, F., Post, W., López Lópe z, M., & Grietens, H. (2021). Participation of children in the child protection system—Validation of the Meaningful Participation Assessment Tool (MPAT). *Child Indicators Research, 14,* 713–735.

Monclús, A.U., Inchaurrondo, A.M., Fernández-Rodrigo, L., & Balsells Bailón, M.A. (2021). The voices of parents and children in foster care. *Journal of Social Work, 21*(6), 1592–1610.

De Mönnink, H. (2017). *The Social Workers' Toolbox. Sustainable Multimethod Social Work.* London, New York: Routledge.

Muench, K., Diaz, C., & Wright, R. (2017). Children and parent participation in child protection conferences: A study in one English local authority. *Child Care in Practice, 23*(1), 49–63.

Munro, E. (2010). Learning to reduce risk in child protection. *British Journal of Social Work, 40,* 1135–1151.

Munro, E., & Turnell, A. (2018). Re-designing organizations to facilitate rights-based practice in child protection. In A. Falch-Eriksen & E. Backe-Hansen (Eds.), *Human Rights in Child Protection* (pp. 89–110). Cham: Palgrave Macmillan.

O'Hare, L., Santin, O., Winter, K., & McGuinness, C. (2016). The reliability and validity of a child and adolescent participation in decision-making questionnaire. *Child: Care, Health and Development, 4,* 692–698.

Olszowya, L., Jaffe, P.G., Dawson, M., Straatmana, A.L., & Saxton, M.D. (2020). Voices from the frontline: Child protection workers' perspectives on barriers to assessing risk in domestic violence cases. *Children and Youth Services Review, 116,* 105208.

Partridge, A. (2005). Children and young people's inclusion in public decision-making. *Support for Learning, 20*(4), 181–189.

Pećnik, N., Matić, J., & Milaković, A.T. (2016). Fulfillment of the child's participation rights in the family and the child's psychosocial adjustment: Children's and parents' views. *Članci*, 399–421.

Pinkney, S. (2018). Competing understandings of children's services. In S. Pinkney (Ed.), *New Directions in Children's Welfare. Professionals, Policy and Practice* (pp. 51–81). London: Springer Nature.

Pölkki, P., Vornanen, R., Pursiainen, M., & Riikonen, M. (2012). Children's participation in child protection processes as experienced by foster children and social workers. *Child Care in Practice, 18*(2), 107–125.

Rap, S., Verkroost, D., & Bruning, M. (2019). Children's participation in Dutch youth care practice: An exploratory study into the opportunities for child participation in youth care from professionals' perspective. *Child Care in Practice, 25*(1), 37–50.

Rogowski, S. (2020). Managers, managerialism and social work with children and families: The deformation of a profession? *Practice, 23*(3), 157–167.

Russ, E., Lonne, B., & Lynch, D. (2020). Increasing child protection workforce retention through promoting a relational-reflective framework for resilience. *Child Abuse and Neglect, 110*(3), 104245.

Saar-Heiman, Y., & Gupta, A. (2020). The poverty-aware paradigm for child protection: A critical framework for policy and practice. *British Journal of Social Work, 50*, 1167–1184.

Sandberg, K. (2018). Children's right to protection under the CRC. In A. Falch-Eriksen, & E. Backe-Hansen (Eds.), *Human Right in Child Protection: Implications for Professional Practice and Policy* (pp. 15–38). Cham: Palgrave Macmillan.

Schmidt, J., Niemeijer, A., Leget, C., Trappenburg, M., & Tonkens, E. (2020). The dignity circle: How to promote dignity in social work practice and policy? *European Journal of Social Work, 23*(6), 945–957.

Schoch, A., Aeby, G., Müller, B., Cottier, M., Seglias, L., Biesel, K., Sauthier, G., & Schnurr, S. (2020). Participation of children and parents in the Swiss child protection system in the past and present: An interdisciplinary perspective. *Social Sciences, 9*(8), 1–19.

Seim, S., & Tor Slettebø, T. (2017). Challenges of participation in child welfare. *European Journal of Social Work, 20*(6), 882–893.

Shier, H. (2001). Pathways to participation: Openings, opportunities and obligations. *Children & Society, 15*(2), 107–117.

Skivenes, M. (2020). *Why Don't Children Participate?* https://discretion.uib.no/why-dont-children-participate/

Staudt, M., Lodato, G., & Hickman, C.R. (2012). Therapists talk about the engagement process. *Community Mental Health, 48*, 212–218.

Stokes, J., & Schmidt, G. (2012). Child protection decision making: A Factorial analysis using case vignettes. *Social Work, 57*(1), 83–90.

Strolin-Goltzman, J., Kollar, S., & Trinkle, J. (2010). Listening to the voices of children in foster care: Youths speak out about child welfare workforce turnover and selection. *Social Work, 55*(1), 47–53.

Strömpl, J., & Luhamaa, K. (2020). Child participation in child welfare removals through the looking glass: Estonian children's and professionals' perspectives compared. *Children and Youth Services Review, 118*, 105421.

Tisdall, E.K.M. (2016). Subjects with agency? Children's participation in family law proceedings, *Journal of Social Welfare and Family Law, 38*(4), 362–379.

Toros, K. (2021a). A systematic review of children's participation in child protection decision-making: Tokenistic presence or not? *Children & Society, 35*(3), 395–411.

Toros, K. (2021b). Children's participation in decision-making from child welfare workers' perspectives: A systematic review. *Research on Social Work Practice, 31*(4), 367–374.

Toros, K., & Falch-Eriksen, A. (2021). "I do not want to cause additional pain …" – Child protection workers' perspectives on child participation in child protection practice. *Journal of Family Social Work, 24*(1), 43–59.

Toros, K., & LaSala, M. (2019). Child protection workers' understanding of the meaning and value of self-reflection in Estonia. *Reflective Practice, 20*(2), 266–278.

Toros, K., Tiko, A., & Saia, K. (2013). Child-centered approach in the context of the assessment of children in need: Reflections of child protection workers' in Estonia. *Children and Youth Services Review, 35*(6), 1015–1022.

Walsh, K. (2020). The *Development of Child Protection Law and Policy. Children, Risk and Modernities*. London, New York: Routledge.

Whittaker, A. (2018). How do child-protection practitioners make decisions in real-life situations? Lessons from the psychology of decision making. *British Journal of Social Work, 48*, 1967–1984.

3 Professional Child Protection and the Child's Freedom of Expression

Asgeir Falch-Eriksen

Today, human rights carried by children through the United Nations Convention on the Rights of the Child (CRC) constitute the dominant set of norms for Child Protection Services (CPS) from one country to the next and across the globe. In total, it comprises a comprehensive norm-set, and where each right carries a claim to legitimacy from within a general human rights standard (Falch-Eriksen, 2012, 2018). No norm-set has achieved a more significant amount of support in either the academic field of research or the particular public service that the CPS provides. Equally, countries not only report their activity regarding the implementation and enforcement of the CRC (cf. CRC Art. 44 on country reports), become indexed and ranked according to how they are embedding, implementing, and enforcing rights (Child Rights Index, KidsRights, Realisation of Children's Rights Index and similar), but has very often implemented rights of the child directly into regular law (Berrick et al., 2016, 2022; Gilbert et al., 2011).

In the effort to make sure children carry rights in a real sense, do the signatory to the convention, or the ruling government, know what is implied by a human rights ethos or standard and that they have obligated themselves to enforce? Do the government know what child rights mean when they embed the human rights standard into public policies or decision-making in public services? Do children have an actual ability to raise a rights claim or have the government a coherent approach to including children as rights claimants? Do children even know what their rights entail, and, provided they do, do what they know about their rights correspond to a human rights standard? Although rights of the child, and especially fundamental rights that children carry and that a government have a duty to enforce, have a more significant potential of developing a more clear-cut jurisprudence in societies that are polarised between majorities and minorities, and where rights become a far more active role in decision-making and court-proceedings. Countries that experience a higher level of agreement across

DOI: 10.4324/9781003150688-3

the political spectrum still have a duty to understand any child's rights equally, both coherently and substantively, across public practices and care contexts to ensure rightful claims are met whenever needed.

By signing the CRC, it becomes a public promise to the rights-holders to enforce human rights so that rights-based practices do not differ too much from one CPS office to the next, from one municipality to the next, and even from one country to the next. Having human rights practices in general, and especially on street level where decisions must be tailored to each child's care context, there is a need to develop a human rights rationale, or a theory, that connects the human rights ethos to the practical context of its application. We need to, and by paraphrasing Kant, develop rational principles to guide the understanding of rights and provide rights with "brains" (Kant, 2006).

A pivotal demand to rights-based professional practices in the CPS, following the CRC, is that individual rights of children are distributed to each child equally and enforced by public services according to a principle of equality and according to a coherent substantive normative-legal approach to human rights (Dworkin, 2013). Article 12 of the CRC is a right each child carries. It stipulates a right of the child to express itself in casework that affects them and that what that child chose to express freely must be given due weight according to the maturity and age of the child. This right is carried irrespective of public services. So each public service must answer this particular right equally and follow a coherent normative-legal approach to human rights. The CRC is even more specific and clarifies that this right relates to all administrative and judicial proceedings, which makes this right in particular influential and a defining trait of most CPS practices as it is a public service and a system of administrative proceedings:

> …the child shall in particular be provided the opportunity to be heard in any judicial and administrative proceedings affecting the child, either directly, or through a representative or an appropriate body, in a manner consistent with the procedural rules of national law.
>
> (Art. 12.2)

As these proceedings lead up to CPS acting to provide protection and care for the child, Art.12 fuels substantially into Art. 3.1, and which demands decision-making have the child's best interests as a primary consideration. Since Art. 12 presupposes that the child knows what it can freely express its opinion is about, and that Art. 12 thereby presupposes the child is informed of the matter at hand, what the child can argue is its interests, and what the child itself would say is in its own best interests. Some version of this approach to practice is something most countries in the world have obligated themselves to strive for, implement, and enforce by ratifying the CRC.

In this chapter, I will attempt to explain how we can understand the basic building blocks of a rights-based professional practice according to CRC Art. 12, namely, to argue the case of a normative-political approach to CRC Art.12. The aim is to provide a theoretical backdrop and rights-based approach to organising professional practice within CPS. This chapter will not discuss this approach against alternative theories that have a human rights ethos as a point of departure, not that this is not fruitful, but because the idea is to merely suggest one version of a more comprehensive approach to Art.12. practices within the CPS.

Constitutional Rights, Optimisation Requirements, and Professional Practice

Children carrying the rights of the CRC are provided equal protection against unlawful or illegitimate interference into their lives. Speaking about protection against unlawful interference is a version of speaking of negative rights as freedoms (See Berlin, 1958), or fundamental rights when transferring the discussion on rights from adults to children. Many, but not all of the CRC rights, are in this regard negative rights, namely that they are protections against unlawful or illegitimate interference on the one hand and become a special type as they apply to the lives of children on the other. These rights are carried against the state, and where the state must enforce the rights (Marshall, 1950).

Although human rights are not always formally embedded in national constitutions or even in regular legislation, individual human rights need to be enforced as constitutional to make sure that each carrier of rights, that is, each child citizen, is bestowed an equal number of rights, that the rights carry equal meaning and that the different protections rights are intended to instil becomes enforced against every possible infringement equally. Constitutional rights having precedence is also why we refer to negative rights as fundamental compared to regular law (Alexy, 2009). This draws on the insight that certain types of societal norms cannot be broken and that these norms, as rights, become a precondition for the legitimate rule of law (Habermas, 1996). The enforcement of negative rights becomes a precondition for legitimate majority rule or threats from other entities that can violate the integrity of the person who carries rights. Only by being enforced as constitutional and taking precedence to regular law can rights safeguard each child from unlawful interference (Falch-Eriksen, 2018).

The negative rights of the CRC provide a wide range of interpretations and do not constitute clear-cut commands that are easily enforced. The rights are often vague and indeterminate (Elster, 1987; Mnookin, 1975). Borrowing from Robert Alexy, we can rather speak of rights as principles that carry an optimisation requirement (Alexy, 2014). Although negative rights carry an optimisation requirement and must be enforced across a wide range of legislation and casework, as principles of this kind, professional rights-based practice become challenged to ensure equal cases are treated equally, and unequal cases are treated unequally as the rule of law prescribes.

For each rights claim raised towards the CPS, a fundamental principle of equality must be maintained throughout professional practices. To Dworkin, which I will lean towards here, the principle of equality, or the right to equal treatment and non-discrimination, is "axiomatic" to a system of rights altogether (Dworkin, 2013). Equal treatment and non-discrimination is a prerequisite to rights-based practices, albeit those raising the claims are often children with variable experiences and different circumstances of care or often carry relevant inequalities from one child to the next that must be allowed to influence decision-making. As rights are held by each unequal child equally, each child must also be optimised equally by way of the rights they carry, which often, then, would lead to unequal treatment from one child to the next. Herein lies the advantage of rights maintaining an optimisation requirement towards its enforcement. Each child within the CPS must be addressed professionally to tailor decision-making to their potentially unique rights claims.

The demand towards equal treatment of equal cases, and the corollary unequal treatment of unequal cases, is fundamental to the rule of law and is often connected to a principle of law (Alexy, 2014; Habermas, 1996). Rules are needed for collective coordination and decision-making, and they need to apply equally to all affected by the legislation. Today, it is an insight visible from country to country and court-room to court-room by the blindfold of Lady Justice, namely, that individuals who raise a rights claim should be treated equally unless their rights claim differ in ways that are relevant to meet the claim, and then these cases must be treated unequally (Aristotle, 1954). Although situated on a street level, facing their clients in their daily lives, professional practitioners within the CPS carry the public duty not only to ensure that the child's rights are not violated, but in cases where they are violated, intervene in such a manner that upholds, enforces, and develops a practice that is aligned with a principle of law. Street-level professionals in public service such as the CPS is demanded, from a constitutional rights-based point of view, to enforce rights equally, which in many respects simply considering each case in its own right and considering how to tailor practices to answer each particular child's rights claim. Hence, CPS professionals carry this blindfold too, especially in matters pertaining to rights that must be optimised by professional judgment, also referred to as discretion (Falch-Eriksen & Backe-Hansen, 2018b).

Upholding a fundamental principle of equality has ramifications for professionals' ability to evaluate and separate equality and inequality or inequality of one case from what has been deemed equal among others (See Alexy, 2009). Therefore, children's cases that are evaluated as equal are treated equally, whereby unequal treatment must be justified by giving valid reasons for differences in treatment. Equality thereby presupposes different treatment whenever cases are unequal. Which they often are. In CPS practices, most casework involves children with very diverse background conditions. To ensure that each right is enforced according to a principle of equality, the inequality from one case to the next needs to correspondingly lead to unequal decision-making among professionals.

The Human Rights Standard

Once the approach to professional rights-based practice has incorporated a precondition that a principle of equality backs each right a child carries, we know that each rights holder must be addressed through an optimisation requirement guiding professional practice; the next step is to answer, "equality of what"? In this book and this chapter, the answer to this question is the normative-political cosmopolitan ethos belonging to human rights and how international human rights norms, as they form a system of rights chiselled out by the United Nations, can guide the professional practice of the CPS (Falch-Eriksen & Backe-Hansen, 2018a; Freeman, 2009; Haugli et al., 2019).

The Preamble to the Universal Declaration of Human Rights (UDHR) has become a key reference point for human rights instruments, widely seen as an origin document for international human rights (Habermas, 2010). Although it is only a declaration, it resonates with the basic principles of a human rights ethos and has thus become a reference point for all other human rights instruments. We will focus on the following recognition made by the UDHR about…

> …the inherent dignity and of the equal and inalienable rights of all members of the human family is the foundation of freedom, justice and peace in the world.
>
> (Preamble)

Furthermore, the Preamble to the UDHR underlines the value of this document as foundational and key to understanding the aim of human rights and how to deduce human rights from a "common standard of achievement" for mankind, as it is stated in the Preamble. As we will treat UDHR as a lead source of a human rights standard, we can use such a standard as a principal anchor point to construct theoretical propositions to what rights-based professional practice entails. Developing a deeper understanding of rights-based practice is a necessary stepping-stone to acquire an adequate understanding of how CRC Art. 12 works throughout the CPS' practice domain.

To this end, safeguarding each person's dignity from unlawful, harmful, and illegitimate interventions serves as the first essential building block to understanding how professional rights-based practise becomes directed. In doing so, we need a concept of dignity to work for us, aligning with a human rights ethos. Also, denying individual rights correlates to denying the inviolable character of individual integrity (Freeman, 2011). Although there are other ways to approach dignity, and interesting from a more philosophical perspective, dignity is key to unveiling how rights work that is the point here (see widely different approaches in, e.g. Habermas, 2010; Waldron, 2013). The concept of dignity will thereby be applied as both pragmatic and political in this chapter, albeit first inspired by Kant's reflections on what constitutes dignity:

> In the kingdom of ends, everything has either a PRICE, or a DIGNITY. What has a price can be replaced with something else, as its equivalent; whereas what is elevated above any price, and hence allows of no equivalent, has a dignity.
>
> (Kant, 2013)

In Kant's line of argument, dignity is granted through rights to each person. By doing so, we elevate each individual to have "no equivalent", and simultaneously recognise that protection against interference must (Habermas, 2010) not become an obstacle towards the character of each individual's dignity, which implies corresponding protection of their autonomy, or freedom, of each person to act out what their dignity prescribes. Denying a person their reason to guide it would coerce this person from acting according to what would make the person have "no equivalent". Liberty, then, is grounded in the freedom each person would need to fulfil the unique personhood that person itself had an interest in becoming or pursuing. This access to an individual right to pursue one's dignity calls for a demand to the legitimacy of law to maintain a fundamental right to individual freedom through law. Dignity, then, first of all…

> …performs the function of a seismograph that registers what is constitutive for a democratic legal order, namely, just those rights that the citizens of a political community must grant themselves if they are to be able to respect one another as members of a voluntary association of free and equal persons.
>
> (Habermas, 2010)

We could also refer to a more modern concept of dignity, as Rawls refers to individuals carrying equal dignity through each satisfying "the conditions of moral personality" (Rawls, 1999). The safeguard of dignity is thereby intrinsically linked to a fundamental right to liberty, where the violation of an individual's liberty also becomes a violation of that person's dignity due to the infringements laid upon that person's right to act according to their "moral personality" and self-interest. Consequently, rights developed with dignity as a point of departure is the compromise that makes sure liberty can be acted upon in such a manner that it does not infringe upon others' acting on the same fundamental right to liberty.

The human rights standard becomes oriented by securing dignity and that each person is enabled to act upon their self-interest. Hence, the standard establishes a normative order set to defend the equal worth of each individual's dignity, where inalienable rights are bestowed to each "member of the human family" (UNDP, Art.1). Each human right, then, and across human rights instruments, can be seen as derivations from and specifications of what is needed to safeguard human dignity and the inviolable integrity of each person. Protecting each individual's dignity becomes the moral aim of human rights (Habermas, 2010). By using the dignity of the human person as a lever and applying the logic from how human rights are derived and specified from it, we can utilise a human rights standard that uses the same rationale but to guide the development of rights-based professional practice.

Using dignity professionally in practice in this manner, and in combination with different rights embedded across human rights instruments, we can specify how human rights must be applied more accurately into each right's claimant unique situation and reach the aim of securing that person's dignity. Provided proper institutional arrangements of the CPS, which utilises the concept of dignity to practice according to a human rights standard, the link has become established by the standard between the aim of human rights, the human rights themselves, and how to practice according to them. This implies that practices within the CPS do not depend on the positive enforcement of the rights norms of the CRC alone, as they are articulated explicitly in the human rights instruments, but can be expanded on and elaborated to be correctly and professionally applied to particular contexts, to specific claims, developing practices based on a human rights standard. Individual dignity can thus be seen as the moral source of both human rights and rights-based practices and as a tool to separate legitimate professional practices from illegitimate practices, legitimate decision-making from illegitimate decision-making. By tapping into what is needed to safeguard dignity, we can deduce what human rights imply in more particularistic settings, especially concerning making rights work contextually on street level through professional practice. Dignity, then, is the conceptual hinge, as Habermas would call it, between morality and law, and from law down to street-level practices designed to enforce the rights of each child (see Habermas, 2010).

To illustrate, by filtering CRC Art.12 through the insights that it is set to secure the dignity of each child, we can argue for a far more accurate understanding of what this rights norm entail in each CPS context. We then know why the child is to express their views in cases that affect them in the CPS, namely, to safeguard that decision-making optimise securing the child's dignity and corollary self-interest through each decision. Hence, the human rights standard works to qualify professional decision-making to be in the child's best interests.

The Human Rights Standard and Indivisibility of Human Rights

In CPS practices, to ensure that each child's dignity is secured as a matter of right, each child's rights presuppose professionalism that through rights-based approaches tailor decision-making that answers the specific rights-claim of each child and simultaneously enforces a professional ethics based on an egalitarian universalism justified by the human rights standard. The human rights standard can also be used as a key to understanding what is meant by the indivisibility of human rights. For rights-based practices to work, they must be distributed according to a principle of equality. From the outset, one specific right must be presupposed to mean the same from one practice to the next, namely carrying the same core objective of securing the dignity of each person. To obtain such an aim throughout CPS practices, we can understand each right carrying a dualism between the normatively embedded human rights standard on one side and what rights-norms implies empirically on street level on the other. Here, we borrow from what Habermas refers to as the moral-legal Janus face of human rights, where the positivisation of rights is mediated through the concept of dignity, and which we now push further into the application and enforcement of rights through professional practice (Habermas, 1996, 2010).

To understand how the human rights standard works to develop professional practices, such rights-based practices must uphold any relevant human rights and how they are interconnected. In this manner, the concept of dignity is presupposed to the extrapolation of any right or any rights-based practice, and where the concept of dignity becomes the source of everyone's rights and how their claims must be addressed in each case. Therefore, rights become enforced as the answer, or expression, to a series of dimensions to what is meant by securing the "dignity" of each person.

To secure the "dignity" of each child, the human rights standard must be upheld on a fundamental level, i.e. on a constitutional level. What is implied by a constitutional level is that no person or entity, nor any democratic assembly can act or threaten the dignity of any one individual on the one hand, and on the other, the duty on the state itself to make sure that rights are enforced in a correct manner (Barber, 2018). Hence, politics, law-making, policy-making, and professional practices, as the final joint in a democratic chain-of-command, becomes not only restricted by a legal-normative conception of legitimacy embedded in the human rights standard but also becomes a part of the constitutional architecture of securing the enforcement of individual rights.

Basic types of rights within a constitutional system of rights are negative rights, membership rights, and the right to legal remedies (Dworkin, 2013; Habermas, 1996; Marshall, 1950). These three, and how they are ordered, are interdependent and constitute a constitutional guarantee of individual freedom and integrity and, "in a word, there is no legitimate law without these three" (Habermas, 1996). Only by securing constitutional protection of negative rights will freedom from interference and the freedom to pursue whatever aim you want to be granted, and any legislation, policy, professionalism or any interaction in general in breach of basic rights will be a breach in any individual's fundamental rights. Hence, basic to constitutionalism is the need to secure the liberty of each individual as a matter of right, which is a space for personal autonomy, and for individuals to pursue a life following their self-interests in conjunction with all others having the same particular right. This primary tenant of liberal political theory has its roots back to Locke and Kant but is generally seen today as prerequisites of a modern liberal constitutional democracy (Habermas, 1996; Rawls, 1993).

Children, as adults, carry negative rights; children too have a right to protection of their dignity from unwanted infringement. Whenever administrative proceedings affect them, this becomes interference into their lives with potential violations of their interests. We could even argue that children in the system of CPS are in particular threatened of having their dignity violated as their rights claims are about protection from violence. Consequently, Art. 12, in combination with CPS being mandated to *protect* the child from harmful and violent interference from parents and public interference by the CPS, calls for justification of decision-making to claim that the decision will be in the child's best interests. As CPS carries a constitutional duty to enforce the rights of the child, and the child's best interests, decisions must become informed by what a child feels, needs, or does not need in their care context. Although a child cannot live a life on their own, and make decisions on their own care, because it is a child, it still is a potential violation of their dignity whenever administrative and judicial proceedings are underway by the CPS that do not include the child into decision-making processes.

Also, as the negative rights of the child cannot be revoked by CPS due to its constitutional character, negative rights, and what is meant by liberty must be understood while developing professional practices to enforce Art. 12, it must become part of how professional knowledge is developed. For instance, enforcing negative rights is different from enforcing welfare rights, implying that CPS is, in principle, not a welfare state service but a particular service aimed at protecting a child's fundamental rights.

Violation of Dignity as Violation of Best Interests

The fundamental right to individual liberty implies a right to pursue one's self-interest and what individual dignity prescribes. A fundamental principle right to liberty, carried by each, can structure professional practice and make sure that practices can only claim to be legitimate if they do not violate the right to pursue one's dignity through self-interest. This is a Kantian insight, and it translates to this topic here as professional practices cannot unfairly infringe on an individual's liberty without threatening the principle of personal liberty altogether. Hence, the right to personal liberty, which is set to protect one's dignity, must be safeguarded before any other right, and which is about following one own's self-interest – the freedom to pursue your conception of the good as Rawls would call it (Rawls, 1999). The legitimacy of professional practice becomes dependent on being interconnected to its claim to uphold a fundamental right to liberty carried by the child on the one hand and not having consequences of impeding freedom upon implementation and enforcement on the other.

To Kant and many modern scholars of political liberalism, individual dignity is the natural source of the individual right to liberty (Habermas, 2012; Rawls, 1999). Individual dignity is obviously also bestowed upon children as a matter of right as they too are moral subjects (cf. Rawls, 1999). The challenge that children pose is that although every child is bestowed negative liberty, in the sense that their liberty cannot be constrained externally (Berlin, 1958), they cannot invoke such freedom positively themselves – in the sense of acting upon their negative freedom. To such an end, they need to develop a moral and rational awareness to act. Rawls picked up on this later and referred to it as acquiring moral powers (Rawls, 1993), or as Martha Nussbaum refers to as the development of each person's moral psychology (Nussbaum, 2019). Going on from the child's negative liberty and acting on such liberty positively calls for the moral psychology of the child to be fully able to act according to self-interest and a concept of justice. Children, then, need to develop the capacity for fully autonomous actions before acting on them. This is something that childhood prepares a child for towards adulthood. Hence, the child has a prospective right to full liberty, both the negative liberty and the ability to act on liberty. To clarify, negative rights secure liberty, and liberty has a negative and a positive side to it, where the negative is the intrinsic liberty of each person, and the positive is the ability to act on such liberty.

Child's Best Interests and the Right to Liberty

During childhood, the child constantly needs attention, guidance, nourishment, comfort, and fun. To Kant, children are unwillingly brought into this world, and for that reason alone, the parents have an obligation to provide satisfying conditions for the child's development. An equal sentiment is to be traced today and embedded in the CRC's Preamble:

> Recognising that the child, for the full and harmonious development of his or her personality, should grow up in a family environment, in an atmosphere of happiness, love and understanding....

During childhood, and as the child develops its capacity for self-determination, the parents must act on behalf of the child, i.e. acting on the child's interests in any given case. Whereas the child has a negative right to liberty, the parents are needed to manage the child's positive liberty on behalf of the child through approximating the child's interests. Now, positive liberty is not to be confused with positive rights either. Child protection is all about protecting the negative rights of the child, which carries both a negative and a positive side of liberty (Berlin, 1958). Positive liberty has to do with acting on liberty in society and participating socially. Social rights, or welfare rights, are not something I will discuss here.

Now, the demands towards CPS, as well as caretakers, are kind of straightforward. The right to personal liberty that the child receives as an adult must be something the child is prepared for and can make use of once adulthood ticks in. This implies that when the personal self-interest of a young adult is set to guide him, it correlates to the personal self-interests the adult had as a child. Hence, the preparedness to act is developed during childhood, foremost by the child alone, but with the guidance and care of caretakers or the CPS. This fundamental point in securing the child's dignity through childhood and into adulthood has implications for professional practices in the CPS. Professional practices cannot ignore who the child was, who it is, and who that child will be through its own volition and best interests when conducting professional decision-making on matters that affect the child.

To illustrate: Once a child is removed from parents' custody, and the CPS replaces the parents, it becomes the public's duty to manage where the parents could not. However, the CPS must have a far more detailed account of the justification of how and why they decide to interfere in the life of the child. To act as parents and become their proxy, the CPS must respect and uphold the child's negative right to liberty while simultaneously alluding to the developmental trajectory of the child stipulated by the child's perspective right to full liberty as an adult, that adult's self-interest and the dignity it carries. Albeit, the professional, can only allude to the self-interests of the future adult, the goal is to raise a claim on what is in the child's best interests here and now by arguing for a decision to secure the child's dignity. Even though such a process would be aligned with rights-based practice, it must be stressed that decisions can never be equal to the child's best interests (Mnookin, 1975). In the process of reaching such a decision that lay claim on being in the child's best interests, it can only be done by observing the child's interests and getting to know the child as stipulated by Art.12.

Professional Practice and CRC Article 12

For professional practices in the CPS to enforce CRC Art. 12, there is a need to understand the type of casework the CPS is handling in connection to the human rights standard. The casework of any child within the CPS is embedded in administrative and court proceedings. Consequently, the child's freedom to express itself in matters that affect them becomes activated the moment the CPS engage with the family, the child, the child's care context, and the child's future. In CPS' effort to enforce its public mandate to protect the child, the child's life is interfered with in a manner that potentially, and most likely, will affect the individual child's dignity, i.e. their moral personhood. To secure that the child's best interests shape decisions affecting the child, the child has the freedom to express itself that the CPS must enforce continuously throughout the case proceedings belonging to the child. Critical to developing an understanding of who the child is, the expressions the child provides must be allowed to become relevant and reflexive, something that demands that the child is informed and allowed time to participate optimally. In doing so, the CPS taps into the individual child's conception of themselves, their interests, their identity and social preferences, and which will not only inform the casework for the CPS professionals but will assist in qualifying decision-making towards the claim on serving what is in the child's best interests.

While enforcing the right constitutes a crucial resource to respect and maintain the child's dignity, and by approximating the child's best interests, the age and how mature the child is can become a challenge as to how their expressions are allowed to shape decision-making. However, no child's expression, no matter the age or maturity, is left to decide on care matters. Each child can only influence and argue their interests, and it is up to the professionals to what degree or whether or not to allow expressions to influence decision-making. Knowing whether or not maturity or age matters can be established once the professional knows the child, their interests, who they are and where the child's developmental trajectory is heading. Not collecting a child's expressions and allowing them to influence decision-making must thereby be argued for and legitimised by the professionals.

To understand how to embed Art. 12 into professional practices in CPS, we first need to understand the source from which this individual rights' normative understanding and reasoning are based in a human rights standard, and that following such a line of reasoning, Art. 12 assist the professional practice in reaching decisions in the child's best interests. Such an exercise will also need to convey how the right belongs to a child with a prospective right to liberty, compared to an adult who can act according to self-interest. If administrative proceedings were deemed in violation of an adults self-interest, the adult could resort to legal remedies. The child simultaneously has and has not the same right. A child has a self-interest under development, and whenever the public interferes, to secure the child's dignity, the child must be asked and be allowed to convey needs, interests, preferences, etc. If a child expresses disdain for specific actions, the CPS has the role of being the proxy of the parents and assist developing the child's positive liberty. CPS can only maintain its course with the child's protests if the child's dignity becomes protected.

The child's lack of ability to act entirely on their liberty rights is key to understanding parents' fiduciary role and professional practices within the CPS. Until a child can act freely, it will need other people's reason to guide actions that are in the child's best interests. As a child expresses itself, those who provide care must remain vigilant in evaluating whether or not what is expressed is reasonable and in line with the child's developing ability to act on positive liberty, to act on a conception of the good, i.e. what is the child's self-interest.

Being a child and lacking the moral psychology to rationally know how to act in their own best interests or how to interact autonomously is the lead cause for developing human rights for children. It is not group rights per se but must be seen as how a human rights standard needs specific rights for children to safeguard their dignity. Hence, although children are excluded from carrying rights in the same manner as adults, which require the person's ability to act entirely autonomously, the aim is to secure the same objective – the person's dignity. Consequently, a child has a prospective right to individual liberty once it reaches adulthood. Until then, the child as a rights holder remains a special case within a human rights system, and professional practices set to enforce rights must be explicitly developed to enforce children's rights. Rights-based practices are developed according to a fiduciary principle that grants professional practitioners within the CPS the duty to interpret and understand the child's expressions and how they align with the child's trajectory towards adulthood, i.e. its dignity.

Conclusion

For CPS to abide by what Art.12 calls for, from the point of view of a human rights standard, it cannot merely listen to the child here and now, or simply participate for the sake of participation, and to "tick off the box" in the administrative system. Nor can CPS practitioners assume the information carried by the child's expressions can be a separate issue altogether from the CPS practices but must allow the child's expressions to assist reflexively in qualifying decision-making to become in the child's best interests. If the child's expressions are not included reflexively with professionals' administrative- and court proceedings, the child has not been included communicatively to express itself in line with what their interests might be. The child must thereby be informed and included in a real conversation revolving around the purpose and aim of the proceedings to provide protection. On a more fundamental level, the aim of enforcing Art.12 for the CPS is to acquire an understanding of how the child's expressions align with the child's perspective right to liberty, i.e. their dignity and future self-interests, and how its future self-interests can inform the interests of the child in the here and now. Art.12 is activated continuously across different practice domains in CPS practices and must be seen interconnected to administrative and court proceedings as the child's dignity becomes affected.

For professional practise within CPS to be rights-based, whereby Art.12 must be enforced coherently on a case by case basis, practice must allow itself to be informed and guided by a human rights standard and not merely act as if Art.12 was a definite rule disconnected from a more fundamental human rights standard. Art. 12 must be enforced and adjusted to every conceivable field of practice together with all other rights that become activated by the case at hand, and the professional must reason as to what is demanded by the case for it to abide by a human rights standard. In this effort, the professional allows decision-making to be guided by the core purpose of human rights: securing each child's dignity. To CPS, this aligns with enforcing the child's prospective right to liberty, which points into the distant future of the individual child – towards the particular child's adulthood and where the child becomes autonomous and receives rights as a full-fledged citizen. This imagined adulthood represents the developmental trajectory of the child's interests and which the CPS practitioner must claim to approximate through decision-making. When the CPS practitioner receives expressions of thought from the child itself, whatever it may be, and what the child assumes is its interests, they can be used to qualify the claim to reach decisions that are in the child's best interests.

Professional practices developed from human rights and embedded into CPS are something that each modern democratic state-system must have an ongoing and reflexive relation to. Human rights, constitutionally secured, discussed, developed, and embedded into professional knowledge and applied in practices, can provide the necessary ingredients and backdrop for designing professional practices that respect and uphold human rights.

Acknowledgement

This chapter is informed by the "Cosmopolitan Turn and Democratic Sentiments" project, supported by the EEA-grant EEA-RO-NO-2018-0586.

References

Alexy, R. (2009). *A Theory of Constitutional Rights* (J. Rivers, Trans.). Oxford: Oxford University Press.

Alexy, R. (2014). Constitutional rights, democracy, and representation. *Ricerche Giuridiche, 3*(2), 197–209.

Aristotle. (1954). *The Nicomachean Ethics* (D. Ross, Trans.). London: Oxford University Press.

Barber, N.W. (2018). *The Principles of Constitutionalism*. Oxford: Oxford University Press.

Berlin, I. (1958). *Two Concepts of Liberty. An Inaugural Lecture Delivered before the University of Oxford on 31 October 1958*. Oxford: Clarendon.

Berrick, J., Dickens, J., Poso, T., & Skivenes, M. (2016). Time, institutional support, and quality of decision making in child protection: A cross-country analysis. *Human Service Organizations Management Leadership & Governance, 40*(5), 451–468. doi:10.1080/23303131.2016.1159637

Berrick, J., Gilbert, N., & Skivenes, M. (Eds.). (2022). *International Handbook of Child Protection Systems*. London: Oxford University Press.

Dworkin, R. (2013). *Taking Rights Seriously*. London: Bloomsbury Publishing Plc.

Elster, J. (1987). Solomonic judgments – against the best interest of the child. *University of Chicago Law Review, 54*(1), 1–45. doi: 10.2307/1599714

Falch-Eriksen, A. (2012). The promise of trust – An inquiry into the legal design of coercive decision-making in Norway. In: HiOA Avhandling: 2012/5, https://hdl.handle.net/10642/1355

Falch-Eriksen, A. (2018). Rights and professional practice: How to understand their interconnection. In A. Falch-Eriksen & E. Backe-Hansen (Eds.), *Human Rights in Child Protection: Implications for Professional Practice and Policy* (pp. 39–58). London: Palgrave Macmillan.

Falch-Eriksen, A., & Backe-Hansen, E. (2018a). Child protection and human rights: A call for professional practice and policy. In A. Falch-Eriksen & E. Backe-Hansen (Eds.), *Human Rights in Child Protection. Implications for Professional Practice and Policy* (pp. 1–14). London: Palgrave Macmillan.

Falch-Eriksen, A., & Backe-Hansen, E. (2018b). *Human Rights in Child Protection : Implications for Professional Practice and Policy*. London: Palgrave Macmillan.

Freeman, M. (2009). Children's rights as human rights: Reading the UNCRC. In J. Qvortrup, William A. Corsaro and Michael-Sebastian Honig (Eds.), *The Palgrave Handbook of Childhood Studies* (pp. 377–393). London: Palgrave Macmillan.

Freeman, M. (2011). *Children's Rights: Progress and Perspectives: Essays from the International Journal of Children's Rights*. Leiden: Brill.

Gilbert, N., Parton, N., & Skivenes, M. (2011). *Child Protection Systems: International Trends and Orientations*. New York: Oxford University Press.

Habermas, J. (1996). *Between Facts and Norms. Contributions to a Discourse Theory of Law and Democracy* (W. Rehg, Trans.). Cambridge, MA: The MIT Press.

Habermas, J. (2010). The concept of human dignity and the realistic utopia of human rights. *Metaphilosophy, 41*(4), 464–480. doi: 10.1111/j.1467-9973.2010.01648.x

Habermas, J. (2012). The concept of human dignity and the realistic utopia of human rights. In Claudio Corradetti (Ed.), *Philosophical Dimensions of Human Rights* (pp. 63–79). London: Springer.

Haugli, T., Nylund, A., Sigurdsen, R., & Bendiksen, L.R. (2019). *Children's Constitutional Rights in the Nordic Countries*. Leiden: Brill.

Kant, I. (2006). *The Science of Right*. Digireads. com.

Kant, I. (2013). *Groundwork of the Metaphysics of Morals: A German-English Edition* (M. t. Gregor & J. t. Timmermann, Trans.). Cambridge: Cambridge University Press.

Marshall, T.H. (1950). *Citizenship and Social Class*. London: Cambridge University Press.

Mnookin, R. (1975). Child-custody adjudication: Judicial functions in the face of indeterminacy. *Law and Contemporary Problems, 39*(3), 226–293. Retrieved from http://www.jstor.org/stable/1191273

Nussbaum, M.C. (2019). *The Cosmopolitan Tradition*. Cambridge, MA: Harvard University Press.

Rawls, J. (1993). *Political Liberalism*. New York: Columbia University Press.

Rawls, J. (1999). *A Theory of Justice* (Rev. ed.). Oxford: Oxford University Press.

Waldron, J. (2013). Is dignity the foundation of human rights? NYU School of Law, Public Law Research Paper (12–73).

4 The Case of Assessment

Child Participation during Administrative Proceedings

Karmen Toros and Rafaela Lehtme

Child protection is a complex and difficult field (Isokuortti et al., 2020; Russ et al., 2020) where one main task is to clarify information and conduct assessments of reported cases of harm (Mainstone, 2014; Vis et al., 2021). As a vital part of service delivery, effective assessment contributes to better outcomes and increased well-being for children in need (Gotvassli & Moe, 2019). In this chapter, a child in need is defined as a child whose well-being is threatened or where suspicion has arisen concerning possible neglect, abuse, or other violation of a child's rights to safety and protection (Lauri et al., 2021). Child protection assessments require accuracy and comprehensiveness when evaluating risks and protective factors and the need for services in order to support the well-being of the child (Dickens et al., 2019). In this regard, understanding a child's life, experiences, and needs is crucial and cannot be done without hearing the child (van Bijleveld et al., 2019).

Child Protective Services (CPS) professionals have a key role in the assessment process. Meysen and Kelly (2018) explain that assessment involves diverse responsibilities and methods with limited reliability for predicting future developments. Ferguson (2017) brings up an important point here – CPS professionals need to keep the focus of the assessment on the needs of the child, so that the child does not, in a sense, become invisible.

Assessment involves the evaluation of needs for protective measures, i.e., whether or not the quality of care is below a threshold of acceptability, and also forms the basis for decisions on what appropriate interventions or measures are needed. Thus, child protection assessment 'is of great importance not only for the child's opportunities to receive help but also for the child's well-being and future development more generally' (Petersen, 2018, p. 610). This again acknowledges the significance of children's participation in the assessment process and the need to allow children to express themselves and be listened to. The exercise of a child's right to be heard is a crucial element of the assessment processes (GC No. 12, p. 7). Nevertheless, children's voices are only partially apparent during assessments and decision-making processes, although studies suggest that children want to share their opinions and experiences (Dillon et al., 2016; Kosher & Ben-Arieh, 2020; Lauri et al., 2020; Mateos et al., 2017). Furthermore, the information collected from children is often incomplete due to the limited time spent engaging with children while assessing their situations and making decisions (Yelick & Thyer, 2019).

Assessment Framework

Social work practitioners consider assessments to be a foundation for child welfare and protection practice (Petersen, 2018; Toros, 2012). Assessments give a better understanding of the child's situation and can be referred to as care diagnostics. It enables CPS professionals to make informed decisions and to respond more effectively according to the best interests of the child. Bouma (2019) outlines a four-phase assessment: identifying, investigating, intervening, and evaluating (cf. Middel et al., 2021). A crucial part of the assessment process includes critical analysis – analysing children's care, their needs, the nature and level of risk and harm, deciding whether the child is in need, and providing support to address those needs (Firmin, 2020). Mosteiro et al. (2018) similarly conclude that more challenging than data collection is the process of analysing and interpreting the data for a holistic understanding of the situation.

In this chapter, we discuss the components of an assessment based primarily on the UK assessment framework (Department of Health, 2000), which has been at the forefront of an international movement to develop a systematic approach to respond to children in need (Léveillé & Chamberland, 2010). The assessment framework has theoretical roots in developmental ecology and attachment theory (Socialstyrelsen, 2013: cf. Karlsson et al., 2019, p. 1878), and is conceptualised as an equilateral triangle with three main interrelated domains impacting the child's well-being: the developmental needs of children, the parental skills required to meet those needs, and the family and environmental factors likely to influence how those needs are met (Toros et al., 2017). The framework is developed based on findings from a range of research studies, theories from various disciplines, and lessons learned from practice to promote a comprehensive approach towards assessments (Cleaver & Walker 2004; Horwath & Morrison, 2000; Milner & O'Byrne, 2009).

Although this framework originated in the UK, specifically England and Wales (Léveillé & Chamberland, 2010), its universal principles are applicable across countries. Within this framework, assessments should be a continuing process, not a single event, and ensure equality of opportunities, recognise the importance of working in partnership with children and families, use an ecological approach, be built on strengths while also identifying difficulties, use an inter-agency approach to assessment and provision, be grounded in evidence-based practices and have a child-centred focus (Department of Health, 2000, p. 10). Countries in and outside of Europe, for example, Sweden, Denmark, France, Estonia, and Australia, have adopted and use components of the framework (see Léveillé & Chamberland, 2010) for effective assessment that comprehensively take into account how the current and long-term well-being of a child is influenced by the interaction between the child's developmental needs, parental skills, and environmental factors (three main interrelated domains). This is also in accordance with the ideas of Lou et al. (2008) who discuss child well-being assessments in child welfare practice through infancy and early childhood, middle childhood, and adolescence to evaluate a child's needs for safety, permanency, and well-being.

In the context of child protection assessment, it is also useful to consider the nine risk principles in children's services, described by Munro (2019), most importantly the first five: the child's safety and well-being have to come first in any situation, decisions have to be made in conditions of uncertainty, harm and benefits have to be balanced in the decision-making process, quality of the practice depends on the quality of decision-making, not the outcome, and the context and circumstances of the situation have to be considered when judging the decision. However, regardless of the specific situation, Cohen et al. (2020) outline the assessment to be family and child-centred, strength-based, inclusive, and partnership-based. They elaborate that a family centred approach views the family as a resource to meet challenges and make good decisions. Similarly, Saar-Heiman and Gupta (2020) discuss incorporating parents' perspectives in assessments and decision-making for knowledge production. All this is in line with the assessment framework previously discussed.

In the context of this book, most importantly, we encourage professionals to adopt more holistic and child-centred views with increased focus on child participation. This approach seems to fit well with the concept of Signs of Safety, which is a strengths-based model adapted for the statutory child protection setting developed by Turnell and Edwards with social workers in Australia in the 1990s (Keddell, 2014). This practical model is embedded with a belief in collaboration, strengths-based practice, and the safety of the child, drawing on solution-focused brief therapy to foster a cooperative relationship between workers and families through eliciting the family's perspective on competencies, existing safety, and goals (Turnell & Edwards, 1997: cf. Toros & Falch-Eriksen, 2021). Several scholars utilise the Signs of Safety approach to engage with families and develop effective worker-client relationships in child protection (Nelson-Dusek et al., 2017; Oliver & Charles, 2015; Turnell, 2004), which is crucial for the assessment process, decisions, and interventions designed to enforce child-friendly practices.

In the light of the above discussed concepts and principles, we encourage professionals to adopt more holistic and child-centred views with increased focus on child participation – advocating for these values is one of the aspiration of this book.

Children's Experiences of Participation in Child Protection Assessment

In the following, we will discuss the findings of an empirical study based on the experiences of 16 Estonian children regarding their participation in child protection assessments. The data was collected as part of the larger study 'Effective participatory discourse: Experiences of participants' engagement in the context of child protection assessment practices', approved by the Ethics Committee of the University of Tartu. All participating children, 5 girls and 11 boys aged 9–17 (average age 12.9), were registered for the child protection assessment with a case plan as children in need of assistance. The interviews were carried out in different regions in Estonia from June 2019 to December 2020. Fourteen of the children were living at home with biological parents, one in a foster family, and one child was in a rehabilitation institution for children with substance-use disorders. In half of the cases, the reason for the child protection assessment was the child's truancy and issues concerning homework, other cases included mainly child neglect, abuse, and parental alcohol abuse.

Perspectives and experiences regarding participation were gathered through in-depth semi-structured interviews covering the following main areas: the first meeting with the child protective worker in the last initiated case plan, follow-up meetings, satisfaction with CPS actions and expectations, and child participation. The focus of the interview was on the children's stories, asking them to reflect, describe, and give examples. Informed consent was prepared and signed by both children and their parents, describing the aim of the study, interview process, data analysis, the use of the data, how children's views contribute to the study, also confidentiality and anonymity regarding records and participants. In subsequent paragraphs, we will elaborate on the empirical results of the study in the context of child participation with references to international research on the topic.

Participation Opportunities and Voicing Opinions

Creating the necessary conditions and encouraging children to participate and express their views is one of the most crucial tasks for effective child protection assessments. This requires the practitioner to focus on the importance of the worker-child relationship and to create an environment for the child to feel able to open up and share their story. Children in our study had various experiences regarding levels of contact from CPS – most commonly meetings occurred from one to three times per week, in one case. from zero to once a week. When exploring the nature of the contact, it became evident that even children who had multiple weekly contacts with their worker, actually rarely had meaningful conversations. Three children (ages 9, 10, and 11) explained that they did not have any discussions with the child protective worker, showing that in those cases Article 12 of the Convention on the Rights of the Child (CRC) was disregarded. Most children reported the worker asking only simple questions about school, grades, and favourite subjects, though two children (ages 14 and 15) described having more meaningful discussions that touched on deeper topics. Children with no experiences of participation indicated that the child protective worker only communicated with a parent.

Despite the widespread ratification of the CRC, international studies, similarly to our findings, indicate a pattern of inability for children to express themselves throughout child protection assessments. Findings from a review of studies (16 studies from eight countries published from 2010 to 2018) consistently indicate that children, regardless of country, felt they were not being asked, listened to, or heard, in some cases even in harmful and unsafe situations (Falch-Eriksen et al., 2021). Findings from a review article based on 16 studies from eight countries published between 2010 and 2018 refer that children consistently, regardless of the country, felt they were not being asked, listened to, or heard, in some cases even in harmful and unsafe situations. Other studies have reached to similar results, reporting that children feel overlooked and even silenced (Fylkesnes et al., 2018). Here, it is important to stress that according to Hart (1992), the goal of children's participation is not for children to always participate fully, but that every child should have the opportunity to choose their level of participation depending on their capacities.

Receiving information from the CPS worker about the current circumstances was also insufficient for children participating in the study. Four children learned about CPS' visit from their parents. One child, while admitting the worker explained the reason for visiting, used the word 'arrogant' and 'uninterested' to describe the overall attitude of the worker towards the child's thoughts and feelings. Other children had no idea about an upcoming visit or the reason for it. Similarly, Cossar et al. (2016) found that children received information from family members rather than professionals. In addition, our findings indicate age discrimination; younger children reported more cases of non-participation, with fewer opportunities to express their views and needs. Various studies indicate a similar trend wherein the capacity and maturity of the child are questioned – younger children are seen as not competent enough to participate, share opinions about the case, or understand the situation and its seriousness (van Bijleveld et al., 2014; Husby et al., 2018).

Benson and Rosen (2017) argue that one possible explanation for the absence of younger children and children's voices in general in child protection practice is related to the protectionist approach – protecting children from harm. This misleading approach is embedded in the belief that children need protection from the burden of difficult conversations and painful memories that may be caused by their participation (Lauri et al., 2021). Fern (2014) emphasises the misleading nature of the protectionist approach, arguing that it often leads to harmful effects, for example, increase in children's powerlessness, as they are excluded from information and refused an opportunity to influence decisions about their lives. Another reason for depriving children of their participation rights is the persistent view of children as incapable of contributing to child protection efforts, leading adults to consider their ideas insignificant (Collins, 2017). Middel et al. (2021, p. 715) provide important commentary here – this kind of a paternalistic view is quite often used under the false understanding that it is in the child's best interest, while in reality it only limits children's autonomy and eliminates opportunities for them to participate.

Consistent with already discussed findings, no meaningful participation was identified from the reports of children in the study. However, one girl and one boy, 15 and 14 years old, respectively, shared their thoughts on seemingly more meaningful contact they had with their child protective worker – discussions wherein the worker asked for the child's opinions, what makes them happy, and likes and dislikes. As the boy outlined: '/.../ We talk about everything. What happened, how things evolved. I like these talks /.../'. In general, children wanted their opinions to be asked and heard, but opportunities to share their true thoughts were scarce. The views and preferences were asked only/mainly/mostly on insignificant matters that had no direct effect on the issues regarding the child protection assessment (e.g., type of candies for Christmas or food). A 13-year-old boy shared his experience in exchanging schools without being informed:

> /.../ I wasn't even aware of this. I did not know I had to switch schools. And just like that out of the blue, I was told that I would go to that other school. And then I asked why I had to change schools. I did not know why /.../.

Children believed that the child protective worker's opinion would over-rule their opinion in any case of disagreement, and they would have to do what the child protective worker said or wanted them to do. This refers to the issue of power and control.

Analysing various models of child participation, Franklin and Sloper (2005) argue that genuine participation requires information about deci-sions, including fully formed options available to them and the implications of those options. This is in line with Muench et al. (2017) who highlight that the assessment process needs to be explained in a simplistic way to children (Muench et al., 2017) – what is happening, why it is happening, how long it will last, what the role of CPS is and how the child is involved. Receiving sufficient information on the proceedings and the child protection system itself is crucial for children in order to understand and make sense of their situation (Schoch et al., 2020). Wilson et al. (2020, p. 104974) found that CPS has a strong focus on children's right to provision which can obscure their other rights, such as the right to clear and understandable information, to participate, and to be protected. They locate a fundamental point here – children's right to protection entails more than physical safety; it encom-passes their emotional and psychological safety, and their overall well-being.

Relationship-Based Partnership

For children to participate, and to express themselves, a certain level of trust is required in the relationship with their child protective worker. Building trust takes time (Pinkney, 2018), and a child's relationship with a professional is considered a fundamental factor here (Arbeiter & Toros, 2017; Kennan et al., 2018). While Korpinen and Pöso (2021, p. 856) elab-orate that a relational view of competence is naturally embedded in child protection, current research shows how practitioners still lack important skills in communicating with children and young (Falch-Eriksen et al., 2021; Toros, 2021). Children in the study were asked about their relation-ship with their child protective worker. They shared their thoughts on how to build trust in a relationship – honesty, expressing interest in the child and their life, more frequent meetings and conversations with the child, and patience. One girl elaborated on the idea of genuine interest by refer-ring to the adult wanting to work with the child:

> She [child protective worker] needs to look credible, meaning not angry, as children will not talk if a person is angry. Also, you cannot have an attitude that the child lies or not to trust the child. She has to have an interest for this child, to show interest in being with the child /.../.

This quotation shows the significance of the way a child is approached by a professional. A lack of trust leads to incorrect information. Children who did not experience a trusting relationship claimed to hide their stories from their child protective worker, also choosing the convenient answers expected by the worker, as this boy elaborated:

> This is how it works, I have to think and consider what to say, so there will be no consequences later /.../ Yes, I think carefully before I say it. I say what they want to hear and what is right to say.

Kirk and Duschinsky (2017, p. 965) believe that practitioners know that relationships lie at the heart of social work practice and that working in a relational way improves outcomes for children. It is important to remember that relationships are important at every stage of the assessment process (Fitzgerald & Graham, 2011; Roesch-Marsh et al., 2017). Collins (2017) refers to the tense and unstable nature of relationships, that needs to be considered in child participation and protection. She states that 'while seemingly contradictory, a child has both agency and vulnerability, which must be recognised and advanced' (p. 34). The quality of the child-worker relationship is acknowledged as the basis of the child protection system, enabling CPS workers to conduct comprehensive assessments and understand all domains of the assessment framework, thus enhancing the quality of decision-making (Cortis et al., 2019). Furthermore, the relationship between the professional and the child is fundamental to ethical practice (D'Cruz & Stagnitti, 2008). Russ et al. (2020) go beyond ethical practice here and see the value of relationship-focused practice also in promoting professional resilience and satisfaction.

Children's Views on Enhancing Their Participation

Children shared thoughts how CPS could and should enhance children's participation in the assessment process. The most frequent advice, from 11 children, was to learn about the interests and strengths of the children. Several children mentioned that their child protective worker did not explore these subjects with them. Getting to know the child through open communication enables practitioners to learn about a child's needs, as this 15-year-old boy explained:

> /.../ Perhaps learning to know the child. It's one thing to ask, how are you doing, but this is not enough. You have to get to know the child, so you can assess what happens in that child's life. This way you can have a better picture /.../ Communication is important. And it cannot be

that you just try to make sense of the child, but you really do it, really learn about the child and talk to the child as with an equal. Lot of adults think that you are just a child, just a child. But I think we are equals or sort of.

Sincere interest in the child was considered a precondition to a trusting relationship. A 14-year-old girl explained: 'If she *[child protective worker] doesn't know anything about the child, what the child thinks of the situation, then she [child protective worker] won't know if her decisions will improve the situation or hurt more'.* She elaborated this thought further by underscoring the importance of talking to the child first, not the parent, by saying that the 'child's voice is the strongest'. Kettle (2018) points out that protecting children is about keeping the child at the centre and at the same time learning about the complexity of the context in which the child lives. The focus on the child and child's needs should not be forgotten. O'Reilly and Dolan (2016, p. 1193) refer to Buckley et al. (2006), who state that children are not always put at the centre of assessments and social workers do not always engage with them in a meaningful way. The findings of our study confirm this thought, as children felt overlooked by their child protective workers.

A 15-year-old boy found the principle of confidentiality of utmost importance. Breaching confidentiality closes the door to a trusting or any kind of positive relationship. Several children shared such experiences. Additionally, one-third of children emphasised the importance of communication when encouraging children to participate. Communication was related to getting to know the child and asking the child's opinion on matters important to them. Here one child, a 12-year-old boy, used the term 'child's state', meaning empathic thinking, relating to child's feelings and thoughts, and asking focused on the child. He also argued that while it is not possible to always act according to the wishes of a child, it's necessary to take them into account. Further, children advise CPS workers to talk to the child about why CPS is getting involved with the child and the family, but in a manner that is understandable to the child. Some of the children proposed using various methods with children, specifically playful activities (suggested by children ages 10 and 12).

Vis et al. (2012) consider communicating with children the basis for efficient child participation. They refer to the CRC, which states children do not need to be able to communicate if they are not capable; instead, the practitioner's role is to learn what is in the best interest of the child however possible. Within the CRC, the age of the child is not specified; therefore, it does not matter how old or how capable the child is thought to be (cf. Toros, 2021, p. 405), the opportunity to express themselves has to be provided. Approach and methods are of importance, as discussed by Flynn (2020), who wrote that professional child welfare workers must work with children in sensitive and inclusive ways. O'Reilly and Dolan (2016) elaborate on the value of using creative and playful methods to access a child's world in an appropriate and comfortable way. In order to improve communication with the child, a friendly approach is most helpful for the child to engage in the conversation. These ideas are in line with children's actual thinking, for example, one child used the word 'gentle' and explained the need for the child protective worker to smile to reduce the impression of the 'stranger intruding the home'. Another boy added that professions should be polite, but not in an official manner. Listening to the child was acknowledged as essential, nevertheless, this was seldom experienced in their time with CPS.

Concluding Thoughts on Meaningful Child Participation – Moving towards Rights-Based Professional Practice

In conclusion, we want to outline several essential points to remember while conducting child protection assessments.

First, we strongly agree with Roesch-Marsh et al.'s (2017) idea of participation as a cyclical and relational process. It is not a single event or one-time meeting with a child. Children should hold a central position in the decision-making process from the beginning, as van Bijleveld et al. (2015) stated.

Second, every child needs to be empowered, especially vulnerable children. Children have reported feeling better if they know what is happening. Information gives them an understanding of the implications of interventions (Balsells et al., 2017). Every person is unique with their own experience, including children, therefore, listening enables practitioners to understand them and create solutions and interventions based on their actual needs. As Muench et al. (2017, p. 51) emphasise, it is crucial to learn and understand the wishes and feelings of children to be able to see the world through their eyes.

Third, simply listening is not sufficient to qualify as participation, as Seim and Slettebø (2017) emphasise. Participation is defined as being involved and having an influence on decision-making processes, which shows respect for the child and their right to have a say in decisions that can profoundly affect their lives (Kennan et al., p. 1986). Listening to children, taking their concerns seriously, and providing options make them feel valued (Bessell, 2011).

Fourth, taking away a child's opportunity to participate neither protects nor empowers the child. Children do need protection, but not from participation (Toros, 2021). Middel et al. (2021) argue that children's rights focused on their protection may create tension with rights that ensure children's autonomy, including participation.

Fifth, since children have limited contact with CPS and few possibilities to voice their needs and wishes, it raises the question: are children considered incompetent? Pećnik (2016, p. 401) argues that 'the right to have the child's opinion heard and taken seriously applies to all actions and decisions that affect the lives of children, without age limit, so it applies to the youngest children as well'. Age discrimination, denial of opportunities, tokenistic, and meaningless participation do not improve the well-being of children (Collins, 2017), nor is it consistent with Article 12 or the values of social work practice.

Sixth, professionals need support through legislation and organisation. Leviner (2018) outlines that the reasons why children should participate and what their participation should achieve are not clear in legislation, nor is the generally accepted understanding of maturity in the CRC (cf. Hultman et al., 2020, p. 305). Hultman et al. make a crucial point here – as a consequence of this lack of clarity, the level of children's participation in protection assessments depends on professionals. Organisational structures and routines should not serve as obstacles to implementing participatory practices in child welfare (Seim & Slettebø, 2017).

Seventh, competence is an essential part of any decision-making process (Korpinen & Pösö, 2021). Therefore, the outcome of child participation depends on professionals' skills and ability to support children's participation while protecting them from harm (Strömpl & Luhamaa, 2020). Every practitioner can, from first contact, begin to enhance a child's participation by listening to and hearing the child.

Acknowledgement

This chapter is informed by the 'Effective Participatory Discourse: Experiences of Participants' Engagement in the Context of Child Protection Assessment Practices' project, supported by the Estonian Research Council, grant number PSG305.

References

Arbeiter, E., & Toros, K. (2017). Participatory discourse: Engagement in the context of child protection assessment practices from the perspectives of child protection workers, parents and children. *Children and Youth Services Review, 74*, 17–27.

Balsells, M.Á., Fuentes-Peláez, N., & Pastor, C. (2017). Listening to the voices of children in decision-making: A challenge for the child protection system in Spain. *Children and Youth Services Review, 79*, 418–425.

Benson, L., & Rosen, R. (2017). From silence to solidarity: Locating the absent 'child voice' in the struggle against benefit sanctions. *Children & Society, 31*, 302–314.

Bessell, S. (2011). Participation in decision-making in out-of-home care in Australia: What do young people say. *Children and Youth Services Review, 33*, 496–501.

van Bijleveld, G.G., Bunders-Aelen, J.F.G., & Dedding, C.W.M. (2019). Exploring the essence of enabling child participation within child protection services. *Child & Family Social Work, 25*, 286–293.

van Bijleveld, G.G., Dedding, C.W.M., & Bunders-Aelen, J.F.G. (2014). Seeing eye to eye or not? Young people's and child protection workers' perspectives on children's participation within the Dutch child protection and welfare services. *Children and Youth Services Review, 47*, 253–259.

van Bijleveld, G.G., Dedding, C.W.M., & Bunders-Aelen, J.F.G. (2015). Children's and young people's participation within child welfare and child protection services: A state-of-the-art review. *Child & Family Social Work, 20*, 129–138.

Cleaver, H., & Walker, S. (2004). From policy to practice: The implementation of a new framework for social work assessments of children and families. *Child and Family Social Work, 9*, 81–90.

Cohen, F., Trauernicht, M., Francot, R., & Broekhuizen, M. (2020). Professional competencies of practitioners in family and parenting support programmes. A German and Dutch case study. *Children and Youth Services Review, 116*, 105202.

Collins, T.M. (2017). A child's right to participate: Implications for international child protection. *The International Journal of Human Rights, 21*(1), 14–46.

Cortis, N., Smyth, C., Wade, C., & Katz, I. (2019). Changing practice cultures in statutory child protection: Practitioners' perspectives. *Child & Family Social Work, 24*, 50–58.

Cossar, J., Brandon, M., & Jordan, P. (2016). You've got to trust her and she's got to trust you': Children's views on participation in the child protection system. *Child & Family Social Work, 21*, 103–112.

CRC (United Nations Convention on the Rights of the Child). (1989). New York: United Nations.

D'Cruz, H., & Stagnitti, K. (2008). Reconstructing child welfare through participatory and child-centred professional practice: A conceptual approach. *Child and Family Social Work, 13*, 156–165.

Department of Health. (2000). *Framework for the Assessment of Children in Need and Their Families.* London: The Stationery Office.

Dickens, J., Masson, J., Garside, L., Young, J., & Bader, K. (2019). Courts, care proceedings and outcomes uncertainty: The challenges of achieving and assessing "good outcomes" for children after child protection proceedings. *Child & Family Social Work, 24*, 574–581.

Dillon, J., Greenop, D., & Hills, M. (2016). Participation in child protection: A small-scale qualitative study. *Qualitative Social Work, 15*, 70–85.

Falch-Eriksen, A., Toros, K., Sindi, I., & Lehtme, R. (2021). Children expressing their views in child protection casework: Current research and their rights going forward. *Child & Family Social Work, 26*(3), 485–497.

Ferguson, H. (2017). How children become invisible in child protection work: Findings from research into day-to-day social work practice. *British Journal of Social Work, 47*, 1007–1023.

Fern, E. (2014). Child-directed social work practice: Findings from an action research study conducted in Iceland. *British Journal of Social Work, 44*, 1110–1128.

Firmin, C. (2020). *Contextual Safeguarding and Child Protection. Rewriting the Rules.* New York: Routledge.

Fitzgerald, R., & Graham, A. (2011). "Something amazing I guess": Children's views on having a say about supervised contact. *Australian Social Work, 64*, 487–501.

Flynn, S. (2021). Untroubling children's identity in child protection and welfare assessment through a postconventional analytic. *Journal of Social Work, 21*(6), 1450–1468.

Franklin, A., & Sloper, P. (2009). Supporting the participation of disabled children and young people in decision-making. *Children & Society, 23*(1), 3–15.

Fylkesnes, M.K., Taylor, J., & Iversen, A.C. (2018). Precarious participation: Exploring ethnic minority youth's narratives about out-of-home placement in Norway. *Children and Youth Services Review, 88*, 341–347.

GC (General Comment) No. 12. (2009). *Convention on the Rights of the Child. The Right of the Child to be Heard.* United Nations. CRC/C/GC/12.

Gotvassli, K.A., & Moe, T. (2019). Bridging the gap – the role of leadership in professional judgement in child protection services. *Nordic Social Work Research.* doi:1 0.1080/2156857X.2019.1694057.

Hart, R.A. (1992). *Children's Participation: From Tokenism to Citizenship.* Innocenti Essays, 4. Florence: UNICEF International Child Development Centre. https://www.unicef-irc.org/publications/pdf/childrens_participation.pdf

Horwath, J., & Morrison, T. (2000) Identifying and implementing pathways for organizational change – Using the framework for the assessment of children in need and their families as a case example. *Child and Family Social Work, 5*, 245–254.

Hultman, E., Höjer, S., & Larsson, M. (2020). Age limits for participation in child protection court proceedings in Sweden. *Child & Family Social Work, 25*, 304–312.

Husby, I.S.D., Slettebø, T., & Juul, R. (2018). Partnership with children in child welfare: The importance of trust and pedagogical support. *Child & Family Social Work, 23*, 443–450.

Isokuortti, N., Aaltio, E., Laajasalo, T., & Barlow, J. (2020). Effectiveness of child protection practice models: A systematic review. *Child Abuse & Neglect, 108*, 104632.

Karlsson, H., Avby, G., & Svendsen, T. (2019). QUAT—a Tool for evaluating the quality of core assessments in child-protection investigations. *British Journal of Social Work, 49*, 1875–1892.

Keddell, E. (2014). Theorising the signs of safety approach to child protection social work: Positioning, codes and power. *Children and Youth Services Review, 47*, 70–77.

Kennan, D., Brady, B., & Forkan, C. (2018). Supporting children's participation in decision making: A systematic literature review exploring the effectiveness of participatory processes. *British Journal of Social Work, 48*, 1985–2002.

Kettle, M. (2018). A balancing act–A grounded theory study of the professional judgement of child protection social workers. *Journal of Social Work Practice, 32*(2), 219–231.

Kirk, G., & Duschinsky, R. (2017). On the margins of the child protection system: Creating space for relational social work practice. *Child and Family Social Work, 22*, 963–971.

Korpinen, J., & Pösö, T. (2021). Social workers' views about children's and parents' competence in child protection decision-making. *Journal of Social Work, 21*(4), 853–870.

Kosher, H., & Ben-Arieh, A. (2020). Social workers' perceptions of children's right to participation. *Child & Family Social Work, 25*(2), 294–303.

Lauri, K., Toros, K., & Lehtme, R. (2021). Participation in the child protection assessment: Voices from children in Estonia. *Child and Adolescent Social Work Journal, 38*, 211–226.

Léveillé, S., & Chamberland, C. (2010). Toward a general model for child welfare and protection services: A meta-evaluation of international experiences regarding the adoption of the Framework for the Assessment of Children in Need and Their Families (FACNF). *Children and Youth Services Review, 32*, 929–944.

Lou, C., Anthony, E.K., Stone, S.S., Vu, C.M., & Austin, M.J. (2008). Assessing child and youth well-being. *Journal of Evidence – Based Social Work, 5*(1–2), 91–133.

Mainstone, F. (2014). *Mastering Whole Family Assessment in Social Work. Balancing the Needs of Children, Adults and Their Families*. London: Jessica Kingsley Publishers.

Mateos, A., Vaquero, E., Balsells, M.A., & Ponce, C. (2017). They didn't tell me anything; They just sent me home': Children's participation in the return home. *Child & Family Social Work, 22*, 871–880.

Meysen, T., & Kelly, L. (2018). Child protection systems between professional cooperation and trustful relationships: A comparison of professional practical and ethical dilemmas in England/Wales, Germany, Portugal, and Slovenia. *Child & Family Social Work, 23*, 222–229.

Middel, F., Post, W., Lópet Lópe z, M., & Grietens, H. (2021). Participation of children in the child protection system – Validation of the Meaningful Participation Assessment Tool (MPAT). *Child Indicators Research, 14*, 713–735.

Milner, J., & O'Byrne, P. (2009). *Assessment in Social Work*. New York: Palgrave Macmillan.

Mosteiro, A., Beloki, U., Sobremonte, E., & Rodríguez, A. (2018). Dimensions for argument and variability in child protection decision-making. *Journal of Social Work Practice, 32*(2), 169–187.

Muench, K., Diaz, C., & Wright, R. (2017). Children and parent participation in child protection conferences: A study in one English local authority. *Child Care in Practice, 23*(1), 49–63.

Munro, E. (2019). Decision-making under uncertainty in child protection: Creating a just and learning culture. *Child & Family Social Work, 24*, 123–130.

Nelson-Dusek, S., Rothe, M.I., Roberts, Y.H., & Pecora, P.J. (2017). Assessing the value of family safety networks in child protective services: Early findings from Minnesota. *Child & Family Social Work, 22*, 1365–1373.

Oliver, C., & Charles, G. (2015). Which strengths-based practice? Reconciling strengths-based practice and mandated authority in child protection work. *Social Work, 60*(2), 135–143.

O'Reilly, L., & Dolan, P. (2016). The voice of the child in social work assessments: Age-appropriate communication with children. *British Journal of Social Work, 46*, 1191–1207.

Pećnik, N., Matić, J., & Milaković, A.T. (2016). Fulfillment of the child's participation rights in the family and the child's psychosocial adjustment: Children's and parents' views. *Članci*, 399–421.

Petersen, S.K. (2018). Parents' experiences of child protection practice in Denmark. *Child & Family Social Work, 23*, 609–616.

Pinkney, S. (2018). *New Directions in Children's Welfare. Professionals, Policy and Practice.* London: Palgrave Macmillan.

Roesch-Marsh, A., Gillies, A., & Green, D. (2017). Nurturing the virtuous circle: Looked after Children's participation in reviews, a cyclical and relational process. *Child and Family Social Work, 22*, 904–913.

Russ, E., Lonne, B., & Lynch, D. (2020). Increasing child protection workforce retention through promoting a relational-reflective framework for resilience. *Child Abuse and Neglect, 110*(3), 104245.

Saar-Heiman, Y., & Gupta, A. (2020). The poverty-aware paradigm for child protection: A critical framework for policy and practice. *British Journal of Social Work, 50*, 1167–1184.

Schoch, A., Aeby, G., Müller, B., Cottier, M., Seglias, L., Biesel, K., Sauthier, G., & Schnurr, S. (2020). Participation of children and parents in the Swiss child protection system in the past and present: An interdisciplinary perspective. *Social Sciences, 9*(8), 1–19.

Seim, S., & Tor Slettebø, T. (2017). Challenges of participation in child welfare. *European Journal of Social Work, 20*(6), 882–893.

Strömpl, J., & Luhamaa, K. (2020). Child participation in child welfare removals through the looking glass: Estonian children's and professionals' perspectives compared. *Children and Youth Services Review, 118*, 105421.

Toros, K. (2012). Child protection assessment practices in Estonia. *Journal of Social Policy and Social Work in Transition, 3*(1), 25–49.

Toros, K. (2021). A systematic review of children's participation in child protection decision-making: Tokenistic presence or not? *Children & Society, 35*(3), 395–411.

Toros, K., & Falch-Eriksen, E. (2021). Strengths-based practice in child welfare: A systematic literature review. *Journal of Child and Family Studies, 30*, 1586–1598.

Toros, K., LaSala, M., & Tiko, A. (2017). Assessment of the developmental needs of children in need: Estonian Child Protective Workers' case reflections. *Child & Family Social Work, 22*(2), 843–852.

Turnell, A. (2004). Relationship-grounded, safety organized child protection practice: Dreamtime or real-time option for child welfare? *Protecting Children, 19*(2), 14–25.

Vis, S.A., Holtan, A., & Thomas, N. (2012). Obstacles for child participation in care and protection cases – Why Norwegian social workers find it difficult. *Child Abuse Review, 21*, 7–23.

Vis, S.A., Lauritzen, C., & Fossum, S. (2021). Systematic approaches to assessment in child protection investigations: A literature review. *International Social Work, 64*(3), 325–340.

Wilson, S., Hean, S., Abebe, T., & Heaslip, V. (2020). Children's experiences with child protection services: A synthesis of qualitative evidence. *Children and Youth Services Review, 113*, 104974.

Yelick, A., & Thyer, B. (2019). The effects of family structure and race on decision-making in child welfare. *Journal of Public Child Welfare, 14*(3), 336–356.

5 Child Protection Workers Follow-up with Children in Foster Care and Emergency Units/Homes

Cecilie Basberg Neumann

This chapter concerns the child welfare service's follow-up of children who are placed outside the home. In particular, I will focus on the child welfare service's implementation of Article 12 of the Convention on the Rights of the Child on children's right to express themselves in any judicial and administrative proceedings affecting them. How children's right to express themselves in their own case relates to the concept of relationship in the child welfare service's follow-up of children placed in foster homes will be a central focus of the chapter. The point of departure for the discussions is that the child welfare service's obligation to fulfil Article 12 of the Convention on the Rights of the Child must be indisputable if we are to assert that the child is a bearer of rights. At the same time, the institutional framework within which social workers are expected to comply with Article 12 and respect children's right to express their views and be heard is such that they come up against a reality that is so complex that it is difficult to see how social workers can fulfil the child's right, given the de facto constraints that exist in terms of time, space and establishing good relationships. In other words, children's right to express themselves in their own case during follow-up in a foster home is a right that can easily be overlooked or put under pressure by caseworkers (CWs) and supervisors working in a busy bureaucracy.

The goal of the chapter is therefore to highlight that the children's right to express their views must be fulfilled within an organisation's framework conditions, using professional tools that enable child welfare officers to do good relational work. I have chosen to use a concrete case, 'Alex', to take a closer look at some of the central dilemmas that CWs and supervisors are faced with when following up children in accordance with Article 12 of the Convention on the Rights of the Child. The case in question is an excerpt from a conversation between a boy who has been placed in an emergency foster home, his child welfare CW and the foster parents. The goal of the conversation was to determine where the boy was to live. Alex

DOI: 10.4324/9781003150688-5

was in the emergency foster home because he had been removed from his home as a result of an emergency care order issued because his mother hits him. I was present as an observer during the conversation. The purpose of describing Alex's case is to illustrate the type of situation that a child can be placed in when a child's right to express his views in his own case and to be heard centres around the decisions that the child welfare service is to make, in this case to decide where Alex is to live, rather than focusing on facilitating the parties getting to know each other before exploring a difficult situation and, finally, making a decision. When the CW is pressed for time and focuses on the fact that a decision is to be made about where Alex is to live rather than taking the time to establish a relationship by instilling security and presenting the topic for discussion in an open manner, she not only runs the risk of disregarding what the child says, she also makes it difficult for Alex to express his opinion. Instead of the situation becoming an opportunity to establish a secure relationship, not just as an end in itself, but as a prerequisite for arriving at a decision that is in the child's best interests, the relationship is reduced to its purpose, namely, to reach a decision.

The argument that follows in the chapter builds on the assumption that the child welfare service's interpretation of its obligations to safeguard these rights, as in Alex's case, entails shifting the concept of relationship away from complexity, reciprocity, and cooperation towards responsibility and the choosing individual, when the child's right to express its views and be heard is to be realised by social workers in follow-up interviews with children in care. The relational aspects are thus displaced by an instrumental application of the rights of the child. This misses the very point of human rights, which is to protect the dignity of the individual, in a situation where the CW's work of establishing a relationship with the child is a fundamental premise for safeguarding the best interests of the child.

Against this backdrop, the purpose of this chapter is to challenge what is at stake, both for the child welfare CWs and for the children concerned, when endeavouring to comply with Article 12 in the follow-up of children in care.

What Follow-up Do Children Placed in Care Receive?

The immediate context of my reflections is follow-up of children living in foster homes and emergency foster homes. The follow-up should safeguard the child's right to be listened to and heard. The child welfare service has formal responsibility for the child's care and thus has an obligation to follow up the child and ensure that he or she is doing well.

The CW's follow-up of the child is an important part of the work of safeguarding the child's rights under Article 12 of the Convention on the Rights of the Child. In Norway, a requirement for four visits per year applies, but the number of visits may be reduced to two a year by agreement with the foster parents or emergency foster parents and the child.

No other statutory requirements apply to the follow-up, and the law neither can nor should provide an exhaustive description of professional practice. The law can define minimum requirements, but it is up to professional practice to implement the laws and rules that we, as a society, have decided to live by. In other words, practice must, taking the child's best interests as its point of departure, aim to fulfil the obligation to safeguard the child's dignity and right to state its views and be heard.

What is at stake if the focus is primarily on the legislation, is that, in a busy bureaucracy, the child's right to be heard and have its views given due weight can easily be reduced to a question of whether follow-up actually takes place, and of the child's choice (Lipsky, 2012). That entails a risk of overlooking the fact that the child's freedom of speech must be safeguarded in and through a complex relationship between the person following up the child, the child's guardians, and the child him/herself, a relationship in which the social worker is the responsible party (Neumann, 2018). Safeguarding the legally defined rights and the activities that form the basis for the social worker establishing a relationship must therefore be interlinked. In my view, relational work is in principle a core activity in child welfare and social work (Garrett, 2013; Richmond, 1917), and the fulfilment of children's human rights in the follow-up context depends on this core activity being recognised as crucial to safeguarding the child's freedom of speech and the child's best interests.

Rights and Follow-up through 'a common third'

Children have the right to express their views and have them given due weight in their own case. The question is how these rights are safeguarded in practice. It is my postulate that good relational work is about the child welfare officer's ability and opportunity to establish 'a common third' with the child (Skjervheim, 1996). Establishing a common third means that the child welfare officer sees it as her job to ensure that she and the child can explore together what the problem complex comprises, instead of the child welfare officer having decided in advance what the child should be concerned with, what the child needs or what should be changed in a case or a situation. Establishing a common third also has a lot in common with what

Annemarie Mol (2008) describes as a respectful and cooperative relationship between treatment provider and patient. She uses cooperation between doctors/nurses and diabetes patients as an example. According to Mol, a respectful and cooperative relationship between treatment provider and patient is characterised by the doctor/nurse acknowledging that the patient has valuable knowledge about his or her own life and body, while neither party is in doubt about the value of medical knowledge for the patient. The treatment focuses on how they can work together to achieve the best possible everyday life for the patient with diabetes-related challenges. The cooperation towards this goal is their common third. Mol characterises it as good care when these efforts succeed.

When child welfare professionals establish a similar respectful and cooperative relationship with the child in their professional practice, they are motivated by an attitude to practice whereby an important prerequisite for a rights-based practice that safeguards the child's right to state his or her views is fulfilled in that they neither put pressure on the child to make decisions regarding the child's life that he or she is not mature enough to make, nor urge the child welfare officer to safeguard the child's right to express his or her views at all costs, which does not comply with human rights either. The child has a right, but not an obligation, to express his or her views. In principle, professional guidelines for social work will fulfil the child's human rights when what is realised in and through relationships aspires to achieve presence, recognition, empathic listening, and a good position in relation to the child (Garrett, 2013). Nevertheless, there are many indications that these guidelines for social work practice are overlooked in the concrete work to realise children's right to participation in the follow-up context. This means that part of the social work practice will end up in a situation where there is a conflict between social work and respecting children's human rights, rather than in a situation where the knowledge that forms the basis for social work shows how children's human rights can be fulfilled in practice.

The 'Alex' Case

This case is taken from my field observations of a follow-up interview in 2015. It took place in an (emergency) foster home between a boy, his CW from the child welfare service and his two foster parents. The purpose of the interview was to find out how the boy was faring and to determine where he was to live. I was present in an observer capacity.

The foster father (FF) is quick to complain about the boy's lack of initiative and poor health. The CW has brought along a package from the boy's father containing some clothes and sweets, and the foster mother (FM) quickly says that the boy cannot eat sweets because it will only run straight out again and is disgusting. It is better that he smokes. The conversation about the boy's smoking continues, and FM says that she would rather see the boy smoking than eating sweets. She emphasises that the boy has to smoke outdoors, however. The boy had nearly set the house on fire. He had been smoking in his room, had thrown the cigarette butt out of the window and straight down into a pile of sawdust. Inside the house, with the boy, FF, FM, CW, and myself present, the conversation about smoking continues, and it emerges that the boy has smoked since he was ten years old. The story about setting the house on fire is repeated. The boy is in his late teens, and the FF comments that he is thin and weak. My impression is that he is quite shy to begin with, but becomes more energetic in the course of the conversation and begins to talk more when FF leaves the room. One of several things at stake is talking about where the boy should live.

CW: Earlier, you said that you consent and want to live with your mum.

B: Yes, but I don't know if that is possible, because we talked about it at first, but NAV refused to help.

CW: It doesn't have to take very long now, because the child welfare service wants to help and will pay for it.

B: I don't know, mum isn't interested in living with dad. She will go back to [country] if she has to keep living with him.

CW: Has she given you a date?

B: Mum is tentative about when. She can't take dealing with dad.

CW: Are you okay with everyone here around the table being here?

B: I have nothing against any of the people here.

CW: Has your mother done anything to hurt you physically?

B: No.

CW: I mean violence, has she hit you?

B: No.

FM: [the boy's name], that's not what you told me.

B: [gives a shy smile] Every now and then she has hit me, when I have deserved it.

CW: So we need to teach your mum other ways of setting boundaries.

B: Yes.

CW: But tell me, how often has your mum hit you?

B: There's no point in talking about it.

CW: Have you ever talked to your mum about this?

B: No, because in [country] there was no time for if, because I was never at home.

CW: Hmm, okay, but we're going to have to talk about this later, not today, but if you live with your mother, it will be a topic, because we want a good situation for you, we want you to get on well with your mother.

B: nods

CW: Is there anything else you worry about as regards living with your mum that you haven't told us about yet?

B: No.

[...]

CW: If I understand you correctly, you would prefer to live with your mother, but you don't think that is possible?

B: Yes.

In the example, Alex is assigned a number of subject-positions by his FF and FM. He is viewed as a slob (has turned turn night into day, does nothing), he is a criminal (steals cars), he is a boy in need of care (thin, weak, needs to be shown that the world can be healthy and sporty and good), and he becomes an informant for adults who want to tell him what his parents are really like and about all the bad things they have put him through (Sudland & Neumann, 2021). Neither of the foster parents has managed to establish a collaborative alliance with Alex. On the one hand, Alex is described as completely impossible, while, on the other, he is expected to take responsibility for his own life, as well as for his mother. He is told in no uncertain terms that, if his wish to live with his mother is to be granted, he must help to teach her that a good mother does not hit children, and he must set aside time to talk to her.

My perception of the CW in this example was that she was good at asking questions and keeping the conversation going, both her choice of words (supportive, as in: yes, I think you should give yourself a pat on the shoulder) and the way in which she said the words were framed by short empathic words and a friendly posture (gentle facial expressions, forward-leaning in the sense of signalling presence).

However, she appeared to be leading the conversation in the sense that she was at the meeting to solve the problem of where Alex was to live, and where Alex was the problem. She was less proficient when it came to exploring the contexts of Alex's experience of his own life and the contexts from which the concerns about Alex and his mother originated. She seemed to be unable to, or lack the time and room to, establish a common third.

Like other social workers' activities, a social worker's work is governed by deadlines and targets for decisions and case progress, which results in a situation where the work of safeguarding the child's right to participation and the child's best interests is at risk of becoming instrumental, which, ultimately, could result in the child being objectified. In this way, it will never be possible to establish a rights-based practice either. The case illustrates how the conditions that she is subject to in her work manifest themselves in the conversation with the boy.

Instead of safeguarding the child's right to express his views and have his opinions taken seriously, as required by law, the CW turns Alex into an object of rights-based thinking.

The starting point for the follow-up interview was that the CW and foster parents were to make decisions in the best interests of the child, but the work done here and now does not appear to be based on a relationship that instils feelings of security and trust. Rather than adopting an attitude signalling openness to explore what would be best for Alex, the goal of the CW and foster parents appears to be to clarify possible futures and choices for Alex as quickly as possible. What, in concrete terms, it means to work in and through a relationship is shifted from its roots in establishing a common third ('this is the issue at hand and we will find a solution together') to a situation governed by the perception that it is the duty of one of the parties (the social worker) to fulfil the rights of the other party (the child). This represents a reduction of the cooperation to finding good solutions, which depends on a good relationship, that can set aside the child's subjectivity and make it an object of rights-based thinking, rather than the child's rights inspiring child welfare practices based on the best interests of the child in a broad sense.

Child welfare practices that take as their point of departure that human rights are indivisible mean in concrete terms is that the practices are based on a principle of dignity, does not appear to be the case in the conversation with Alex.

In this follow-up interview, fulfilment of the child's rights is more of a box-ticking exercise – the CW can say that she has talked to Alex and asked him where he wants to live. At the same time, the conversation does not appear to have safeguarded the child's rights in any real sense. Alex is encouraged to state his views, but he is not listened to.

On the contrary, the CW's safeguarding of Alex's rights is structured around his choice of where to live, but because she is unable to establish a cooperative alliance with him, her efforts in relation to Alex seem to be hollow in the sense that the conversation is governed by her need to arrive at a decision, not his. This means that she is unable to create an atmosphere conducive to genuine participation. The point I am trying to make here is that the relationship must be established in order to gain real insight into what would be in Alex's best interests and what Alex might think that would be relevant to the decisions. The CW's signals that 'we are here to listen to you' will thus appear hollow to Alex. Among other things, Alex is asked to take responsibility for his mother, as well as in relation to the question of where he is to live, while, at the same time, he does not know whether it is actually possible for him to live with her. This makes it clear that it is the child welfare service that makes the final decision.

The Different Follow-up Components

The child welfare service's follow-up of children in foster homes and emergency foster homes is based on the Convention on the Rights of the Child's Article 12 on children's right to be heard, have their views given due weight and participate in their own case, and Article 3, which states that the best interests of the child shall be a primary consideration in all decisions concerning children. These provisions are rooted in the child's human rights being indivisible, and it entails a fundamental respect for the child's dignity. In social work practice, safeguarding the child's human rights with reference to Articles 12 and 3 will entail an obligation on the part of social workers to spend enough time with the child to actually get to know him or her and establish a real relationship. They need to talk to the child sufficiently often and in the right way with a view to establishing a cooperative alliance structured around openness and establishing a common third. That is the opposite of having decided the outcome of a conversation in advance, and it rests on a premise that safeguarding of human rights can strengthen established knowledge of good practices in social work.

The Role and Importance of Article 12 in Relation to Follow-up

Article 12 of the Convention on the Rights of the Child's puts the right of children to express their opinion in matters that concern them on the agenda and helps to ensure that professional practitioners do not forget the child and his or her right to be heard. Furthermore, children have a right to express their views, but are not obliged to do so. Article 12 also specifies that the follow-up of the child's right to be heard and have his or her views given due weight shall take the age and maturity of the child into account. This is an absolute requirement in a social work practice that takes human rights seriously.

However, there are indications that, in practice, professionals have neither time nor room, and possibly not the level of expertise required, to facilitate the child's views being heard. The difficulties in respecting the child's right to participation in practice are not solely due to the institutional framework being insufficient or the relationship between the CW and the child not being good enough, but also to the fact that the child does not know what he or she wants or is not able to decide what would be in his or her best interests here and now. When viewed in light of such a complex reality, the actual safeguarding of the child's right to participation may seem to be manual-based or target-based, as well as instrumental, reductionist and counter-productive, when it fails to also take an open and humble approach to the complex elements inherent in any relationship that requires reciprocity and cooperation, which are necessary in order to fulfil the child's rights and to make decisions that are in the child's best interests.

As Alex's case illustrates, Article 12 is often practised within an institutional framework, subject to bureaucratic interpretations of human rights that create shifts in the concepts of relationship, individual and responsibility, which are rarely discussed in the child welfare service context.

These shifts concern the link between the rights of the child as set out in the Convention on the Rights of the Child, and the practices and lived life that are always significant premises for both the child and the CW, and the surrounding systems when decisions are to be made about the best interests of the child. From a human rights perspective, the point of departure is that it is the lived life that the rights are intended to protect, and the child welfare service's practices must safeguard the child's dignity on that basis. Instead, we see that, in practice, the interpretation of legal provisions often takes the form of manual-based procedures that address and try to regulate what unfolds in actual situations, rather than inviting wisdom, flexibility and the exercise of good judgement when dealing with children and their families. In a child welfare service context, respecting a child's dignity will always be framed by relationships characterised by complex interpersonal interaction, and safeguarding the rights of the child requires time (availability), room (closeness), and knowledge. Although there will be a conflict between the legal ideal and actual practice in most areas subject to legal regulation, there is extensive child welfare research that indicates that it is important to study how children's rights are actually safeguarded (Falch-Eriksen & Backe-Hansen 2018).

Complying with Article 12 involves the whole spectrum from actually talking to the child to questions about how to find out what the child wants. If we assume that the institutional framework conditions give CWs time and room to meet the child, talking to the child still does not guarantee that the child will feel that he or she is heard and taken seriously. Among other things, developing good relationships depends on establishing trust, and on CWs being able to achieve a good position in relation to the child (Ulvik, 2009) and being capable of developing a common third (Skjervheim, 1996), where they can arrive at 'something' together. It is also relevant in this context that the child is an individual undergoing change and growth and that children will not to the same extent as adults be aware of what they need, or of how and for what reason they imagine the life they would like for themselves (Cunningham, 1995). The fundamental challenge that emerges when the child is seen as an individual with rights, is that this view is based on a rationalist understanding of the individual, an individual who makes choices. The premise for this understanding is that individuals make choices and take action in situations where they are aware of the constraints on their choices and the potential consequences of their actions. As shown by Østerberg (1976), this is rarely the case for adults, and probably even more rarely for children.

The challenge, as I see it based on the Alex case, is precisely that the understanding of the relationship and the relational aspect is reduced to a situation where there is a choice to be made, but without the question of what would be best for the boy being a shared responsibility between the boy, the foster parents and the CW, or being something to be explored jointly without any of them knowing the answer in advance. This does not tally with the relational work outlined, where the relationship seems to be based on the child's right to express a view and be heard resting on the CW's obligation to fulfil this right. The concept of relationship is thus based on the responsibility and duty of one of the parties (the CW) to realise the right of the other party (the child) to make a choice. This perspective can be interpreted as reflecting the child being in a position as a holder of rights (Sommerfeldt, 2019), and not, for example, as a child who is a developing, exploring and complex individual who is to enter into an alliance with the social worker. In order for Article 12 to be fulfilled, the *relationship* in this context must be based on an understanding whereby the relationship is based on a reciprocal, patient and forgiving cooperation (Mol, 2008) in which it is the CW's responsibility to safeguard the child and be sensitive to the child's level of maturity. The relational premise for fulfilment of the child's human rights is thus that the social worker keeps in mind that the child's right to express its view as set out in Article 12 means that it is the CW who decides to what extent it is relevant to listen to the child's opinions and whether it is in the child's best interests to do so. In other words, the relationship is highly asymmetrical, as it must be. It is therefore up to the CW to know when and how much to follow-up Article 12. This presupposes that the CW is able to justify the choice of when to follow-up and when not to follow up Article 12. In the latter case, when Article 12 is not followed up, it is a requirement that the CW knows what is in the child's best interests, sometimes better than the child does. In order to be able to do this, she must know the child well, and there is much to indicate that manual-based work methods will get in the way of this relational work, which, in my opinion, constitutes the very core of social work. I will conclude this chapter with some comments on this.

Safeguarding Human Rights and the Core Activity of Social Work. Two Sides of the Same Coin?

Working in and through relationships is regarded as fundamental to child welfare and social work practice (Garrett, 2013; Levin, 2004). Nonetheless, extensive research indicates that, in practice, social work and child welfare work are often pushed into using manual-based methods that annual considerations for client participation and do not allow time to consider or take into account the complexity of human life (Falch-Eriksen & Backe-Hansen, 2018; Munro & Turnell, 2018; White et al., 2020).

It is perhaps particularly through the bureaucratised and manual-based understanding of the safeguarding of human rights that the concept of relationship is shifted in professional practice, from its starting point as the foundation for human and interpersonal exploration of a situation towards cultivation of the social worker's responsibility for ticking boxes on a form in goal-oriented processing of a case. Under this system, it is more important to document that a conversation has taken place and that a decision has been made than what the content of the conversation was and whether the relational premises for good cooperative alliances have been met. If fulfilment of the child's human rights is considered to be based on good cooperative alliances and exploration of a common third, the obligation to safeguard the rights of the child could reinforce work methods that are already deeply rooted in social work's self-understanding instead of having the opposite effect.

References

Cunningham, H. (1995). *Children and Childhood in Western Society since 1500*. London: Longman.

Falch-Eriksen, A., & Bache-Hansen, E. (2018) (Eds.). *Human Rights in Child Protection. Implications for Professional Practice and Policy*. London: Palgrave Macmillan.

Garrett, P.M. (2013). *Social Work and Social Theory. Making Connections*. Bristol: Policy Press.

Levin, I. (2004). *Hva er sosialt arbeid?[What is social work?]*. Oslo: Universitetsforlaget.

Lipsky, M. (2010). *Street-Level Bureaucracy: Dilemmas of the Individual in Public Services*. New York: Russel Sage Foundation.

Mol, A. (2008). *The Logic of Care*. London: Routledge.

Munro, E., & Turnell, A. (2018). Re-designing organizations to facilitate rights based practice in child protection. In A. Falch-Eriksen & E. Bache Hansen (Eds.), *Human Rights in Child Protection. Implications for Professional Practice and Policy*. London: Palgrave Macmillan.

Neumann, C.B. (2018). Embodied care practices and the realization of the best interests of the child in residential institutions for young children. In A. Falch Eriksen & E. Bache-Hansen (Eds.), *Human Rights in Child Protection. Implications for Professional Practice and Policy*. London: Palgrave Macmillan.

Østerberg, D. (1976). *Meta-Sociological Essays*. Pittsburgh: Ducuesne University Press.

Richmond, M. (1917). *Social Diagnosis*. New York: Sage.

Skjervheim, H. (1996). *Deltakar og tilskodar*. Oslo: Aschehoug.

Sommerfeldt, M.B. (2019). Relasjoner mellom barn og voksne på barneverninstitusjoner i Norge Vår tids forståelser sett i et historisk perspektiv. *Tidsskriftet Norges Barnevern*, *96*(3), 172–188. doi:10.18261/ISSN.1891-1838. March 4, 2019.

Sudland, C., & Neumann, C.B. (2021). Should we take their children? Caseworkers' negotiations of 'good enough' care for children living with high-conflict parents. *European Journal of Social Work*, *24*(4), 683–695. doi: 10.1080/13691457. 2020.1805588

Ulvik, O.S. (2009). Children's participation rights: Theoretical and practical challenges for professional helpers in cooperation with child clients. *Tidsskrift for Norsk psykologforening*, *46*(12), 1148–1154.

White, S., Gibson, M., Wastell, D., & Walsh, P. (2020). *Reassessing Attachment Theory in Child Welfare*. Bristol: Policy Press.

6 The Case of Social Rehabilitation

Koidu Saia

Children's involvement in the criminal justice system is one of the largest societal challenges to child protection systems across countries. The impact of the offences is wider, deeper, and more long-term, affecting the child's ability to cope in society here and now, but also in the future, as a result of negative bio-psycho-social and economic implications (Loeber et al., 2003).

The timely and efficient support of children in need of assistance, including those who have already committed offences, is imperative to maintaining and enforcing their rights. It is also a separate objective to ensure that these children develop in such a way that they can reach adulthood and choose a life that is normal and reasonable for all. Dually involved children have committed offences and are simultaneously receiving services from both the child protection services and juvenile justice systems, and they often go back and forth between these institutions (Herz et al., 2010; Hirsch et al., 2018; Tuell et al., 2013).

Dually involved children experience higher levels of disadvantages and have more complex needs than children in the general population (Kenny & Nelson, 2008). They come into contact with the justice system at an early age (AIHW, 2018), and their development of their life path and experiences puts them at an increased risk of progression to the adult criminal justice system once they reach adulthood (Chen et al., 2005). Failure to provide adequate support to dually involved children arguably introduces a systemic weakness that speaks to the lack of enforcement of the rights of children (Cashmore, 2012; McFarlane, 2017). One of the challenges to rehabilitation is to breach the cycle of anti-social behaviour giving birth to more anti-social behaviour, and anti-social behavioural norms that the child could act on. Without rehabilitation, the child will risk developing disconnection from regular social bonds, and rather have more social links with peers who express similar anti-social behaviour (Shoemaker, 2010).

DOI: 10.4324/9781003150688-6

Rights-Based Practice in Rehabilitation

The approach to justifying rehabilitation is known as "state-obliged rehabilitation" (Cullen, 2012; Lewis, 2005; Rotman, 1990) and is based on a version of social contract theory: the moral legitimacy of the state's demand that people refrain from offending is maintained if the state fulfils its duty to ensure that people's basic needs are met. Hence, it speaks to the basic liberal notion that every person has the right to live according to freedom from interference and that the state is constitutionally mandated to ensure each citizens' integrity is unharmed by criminal and anti-social behaviour. Rehabilitation thereby becomes the right to a certain minimum of services for offenders aimed at offering each offender an opportunity to reintegrate into society as a normal human being (Rothman, 1990). In cases of dually involved children, the rights and interests of the child set basic demands for services, and especially as children constitute a special case in that they are not adults. Children, who we can assume have not developed their moral psychology, cannot be held equally blameworthy as adults (Nussbaum, 1997).

One of the main principles of the CRC is to always make the interests of a particular child be a primary consideration (CRC Article 3.1.); it also states that parties shall take all appropriate measures to promote physical and psychological recovery and social reintegration of a child victim of any form of neglect, exploitation, or abuse; torture or any other form of cruel, inhuman, or degrading treatment or punishment; or armed conflicts. Such recovery and reintegration shall take place in an environment which fosters the health, self-respect, and dignity of the child (CRC Art 39).

Modern legal frameworks are often shaped by the knowledge that juvenile offenders, as they are children, are different from adults. As children constitute a special case in the criminal justice system, they need special approaches and interventions that focus on the best interests of the child as a matter of right, assist in reintegrating them into society (Liefaard, 2015), and work to secure their overall well-being (Weare & Gray, 2003). Today, it can be argued that the CRC has provided the lead principles for developing practice frameworks in line with children's rights and the treatment of adolescents who are in conflict with the law. Nussbaum makes a clear case that these rights are indivisible and that their aim is to secure the integrity of each child, including meeting children's needs so that their future health is not damaged, securing education so that the child develops their capacities and eventually becomes a decent, participating citizen in society (1997). However, Ferguson (2013) points out the "theory gap" in the practice of children's rights in the juvenile justice system and the conceptual difficulty in reconciling the dual status and rights of the child: as a child and as an offender (Hollingsworth, 2014).

Rights-Based Practices through Child-Friendly Justice

Child-friendly justice (CFJ) is a concept related to the difference in treatment and in the legal status of children compared to adults, which includes the prevention, training, intervention, and effective assistance needed for children who come in contact with the criminal justice system. In this way, CFJ becomes an approach to practice that affects dually involved children and how these children receive services from both child protection services and the criminal justice system. First and foremost, CFJ rests firmly on the principle rights norms of the CRC, and most notably the rights principle of the child's best interests (Guidelines of CFJ, CoE, 2010).

Hollingsworth (2014) highlights the four following mutually supportive ways to implement rights-based and CFJ in relation to the child protection system: (1) The minimum age of criminal responsibility should be set above the age that we think there will be a risk of permanent harm to children if criminally prosecuted. (2) Restructuring the juvenile justice system to not cause harm to children's development to become full-fledged citizens. (3) Maintaining differences in sentencing children from adults. (4) Establishing a rights-based system of resettlement whenever needed.

An important influence on CFJ development is the guidelines provided by The Council of Europe in 2010 (CoE, 2010). The aim of these guidelines is to seek to ensure that the criminal justice system is always friendly towards children, which implies special treatment of children *qua* children, no matter who they are or what they have done. Hence, through these guidelines, there has been a change in acknowledging the importance of the rights of the child through enforcing the core principles of CFJ in practice, through both judicial and administrative proceedings.

Making the justice process friendly and adapting the justice system to children's needs has become a key priority. CFJ is accessible, age appropriate, diligent, adapted to, and focused on the needs of the child. Central to CFJ is respecting the right to due process, to participate in and to understand the proceedings, the right to a private and family life, and the right to integrity and dignity (Guidelines of CFJ, 2010). The guidelines point out the three Ps of the CRC: rights of protection, provision, and participation. These put forward the notion of justice proceedings, in the broadest sense, being adapted to enforce the rights of the child and respond to their needs. As rights holders, children should be able to turn to the justice system to have their rights protected, and while doing so experience procedures that are friendly, take into consideration their level of understanding, their specific vulnerabilities, their position, and their best interests (Vandekerckhove & O'Brien, 2013).

Despite the fact that CFJ guidelines (CoE, 2010) are not mandatory, they constitute a recommended best practice norm for nation-states for how they approach this group of children throughout their rehabilitation. The CFJ guidelines have received widespread interpretation and application in the European Court of Human Rights (Liefaard, 2015), but their usage is sought and applied elsewhere as well, especially where these children receive services (Wiig et al., 2013). The guidelines describe the legal basis of CFJ, the main definitions and principles that require attention before, during, and after legal proceedings involving children in order to ensure their wellbeing and that their developmental trajectory is on a track away from anti-social behaviour and future criminality. Central to the definition is the "views of the child", which is another way of referencing Article 12 of the CRC. Hence, Article 12 is not only embedded in CFJ, but is imperative to understanding who the child is, and to providing both respect and the guidance children need.

According to CFJ, it is necessary to highlight, support, and ensure full participation in all matters concerning children, take their needs seriously, allow the child to inform decision-making in a manner relevant to the child, and not allow participation be shaped by adults' understanding of what the child might want (Mayall, 2000). If, in the opinion of the specialist, the child's own views and how the child reflects on their own best interests is not sufficiently reliable or not applicable, a justification for not listening to the child must be provided. If not, it would be a violation of the principles conducive to CFJ (Cederborg, 2015). CFJ calls for sensitivity when communicating with the child in legal-administrative proceedings and guides practitioners to take into account the child's trauma, emotional stress, and psychological capabilities in addition to their strengths, need for affirmation, and desire for a path away from their current predicament. In this way, participation through allowing the child to express themselves is considered integral to CFJ (Case & Haines, 2015). The inclusion of the rights of the child into CFJ, especially the active and ongoing participation of the child, indicates the emergence of a new approach to working with children, viewing them not as passive receivers of help or objects in need, but as effective actors in their own lives, and with a right to influence decisions that affect them (Archard & Skivenes, 2009; Sandberg, 2018).

In order to effectively allow these children to express themselves as a matter of right, and for rehabilitation services to understand the interests of the child through their participation, some design criteria should be met (Rap, 2013, 2016):

1   Creating a less formal setting
2   Using certain techniques that are geared towards older children

3 Giving a juvenile defendant the opportunity to give their own views on the case
4 Showing genuine interest in the story of the young person
5 Involving parents in the proceedings
6 Explaining the purpose of the meeting, the procedures that are followed, who the participants involved are, and their roles
7 Avoiding the use of judicial jargon
8 Clarifying the judgement and sentence
9 Contributing to the understanding of the consequences of anti-social behaviour and offences the child has committed

These principles should be prioritised while the dually involved child participates in the social rehabilitation service, the components of which will be introduced in the next section.

Components of Interprofessional Collaboration in Social Rehabilitation through CFJ

Casework involving dually involved children constitutes a complex variety of problems and needs, including interprofessional collaboration and the need to abide by the basic principles of CFJ and to find a solution that can handle the intricacies that result from casework in which multiple sources of competencies are drawn upon (Saame, 2008; Vilgats, 2015). Professionals within child protection services and within the juvenile justice system have shown an increased effort to develop practices of interprofessional collaboration (Center for Juvenile Justice Reform at Georgetown University, 2015, 2017; Lutz et al., 2010). Through this collaboration, each child, according to their needs, can be connected with corresponding rehabilitation programs that cross different professions and knowledge-bases, that professionals believe they will respond well to. In line with this development, there has been an increased focus on approaches to intervention which include community-based, evidence-based, and counselling-focused interventions (Hockenberry, 2018), emphasising personal responsibility and development of social skills (UNODC, 2018). Evidence proves that the more comprehensive and higher-quality is the assistance, the greater the reduction in longer-term juvenile correctional costs (OJJDP, 2020).

Dually involved children must receive proper rehabilitative intervention, and it is their voices which become the key to unlocking successful outcomes by decreasing the likelihood of re-entry into the justice system (Loeber et al., 2003). We now know that punishment is not an effective method to motivate children to choose a developmental trajectory away from anti-social behaviour and criminality. Providing children with knowledge on how to lead a healthy lifestyle and steps to accomplish this goal has become a strategy for successful outcomes, and a focus on children's voices and their ownership of the developmental path becomes central (Bradshaw & Rosenborough, 2005; Maybin, 2013; Murray, 2019). To illustrate, the participatory youth practice framework (PYP, Manchester Centre for Youth Studies, 2021) sums up many of the different ways dually involved children can participate and express themselves through rehabilitation:

1 Let them participate and understand what is happening in their lives by informing them adequately
2 Do not ask "why"
3 Acknowledge limited life opportunities and disadvantages
4 Try to avoid threats and sanctions
5 Help them to solve problems
6 Help them to find better options through understanding the importance of personal choice and independence by empowering life skills and coping strategies
7 Develop their ambitions through nurturing creativity, happiness and helping them to find the core of a meaningful life, social identity building, and positive goals
8 Recognise the importance of children making their own life choices

Case Examples: Perceptions on Participation among Dually Involved Children

Currently, opportunities for children to participate and to express themselves are not a dominating part of rehabilitation practices (REF). This means that practices and measures are not informed by the child's own views, and the child will be made to feel a certain level of confusion or unfamiliarity with the practices they are affected by. Empirically, practices do not follow the CFJ principles and thereby are not rights-based. It is evident that interventions are not focused on reducing recidivism (Snyder & Sickmund, 2006) or focused on creating a positive future for the child that is informed by the child themselves (Hillege et al., 2017).

In the following, I will explore certain key case examples that are relevant from the point of view of children's rights and CFJ. This data is based on research conducted in Estonia in 2016. The rehabilitation team coordinator and the case manager were asked to approach their clients (children and their parents, legal representatives) to invite children to participate in the study. Selection criteria for the children were: the child was dually involved in the child protection and justice systems simultaneously and receiving social rehabilitation services for at least one year, and whose cases demonstrated various levels of positivity and complexity. All the children who participated (3 boys and 3 girls, ranging in age from 10 to 17 years old with a mean age of 13.4) had a current social rehabilitation plan. Three were living at home with both parents (none with both biological parents) and three with a single parent. Experiences were gathered through in depth, semi-structured interviews, which lasted 25–45 minutes. Four interviews were conducted in Estonian and two in Russian. Those conducted in Russian were transcribed and translated into Estonian by two graduate students. In all case examples, interprofessional collaboration was present, as the complexity of the child's challenges was too great for one singular profession to solve.

Importance of Trust – Children Tend to Test Their "Professional Friends"

We know that children who are listened to also learn to trust service professionals, at least if these professionals meet the children over time (Toros & Falch-Eriksen, 2021; Toros et al., 2018). The professionals that "pass" the test, and that the child trust, have the potential to provide guidance that the child will listen to and act upon. Trust therefore becomes a precondition for children to take professionals' advice and guidance seriously. Children would thereby prefer to have professionals that recognise them as socially competent, relevant actors who can discuss and solve problems. Younger professionals are more likely to be trusted and chosen to be a "professional friend" (Lauri et al., 2020). Children see younger professionals as more able to understand their problems. Case managers and rehabilitation team members should recognise these preferences and identify opportunities to link children with specialists who can meet these preferences.

Taking Responsibility for One's Own Life and Impact of Friends

Dually involved children find managing relations with their "old, bad" friends and keeping agreements with the rehabilitation team very challenging. They note that it takes courage to build new relationships and let old friends know about the changes in their lives, even with the understanding that this is necessary for moving on and achieving newly set goals. Children often need help with finding ways to cope with complicated relations with their peers and formal network members. Children desire approval from friends, parents, and persons whom they trust and respect. Moreover, they need to overcome old habits. This is a great change for most children involved in rehabilitation services. The child becomes a primary source of information on mapping what needs to change as well as creating a new and better path for the future.

The Context for Participation Must Be Perceived as Safe

Most children who are in need of rehabilitation services lack empowering relationships and supportive informal and formal networks. Social rehabilitation by its nature is closely linked with communication and networking within the child's social network, including parent(s) or grandparents, and friends. Building and rebuilding bridges with formal and informal networks is a focus of rehabilitation services that can help embed the child in a safe social environment once the rehabilitation comes to an end. In most cases, "normal" supportive network ties have been damaged and do not function in a helpful manner. The reasons vary, but the need is the same – to help repair or develop meaningful and important relationships as resources for children and families.

Children receiving social rehabilitation services also value consistent, trust-based information sharing as well as the professional's role in establishing new societal links with the child in a safe environment. The conception of safety is thereby something the professional must be able to tap into and get to know in order to safely navigate how the child's re-entry into society occurs. Professionals must communicate with the child to understand the child's conception of safety is and what it consists of. The quality of the worker-child relationship is vital to identifying the child's best interests, their main needs as well as past and present influences on their lives. This includes mapping the child's main network and key persons in their lives and the barriers family members face in living healthier, more productive lives.

"The Helper Has to Believe in Me!"

Children who are required to participate in rehabilitation services, which can also be referred to as a set of administrative or service procedures, will be able to grasp that certain changes need to be made. In order to do so, they need professionals to believe in them, to respond to them, and to assist them in a manner that motivates them to continue. This can only happen with open communication and opportunities for the child to express themselves throughout the rehabilitation process. Correspondingly, a part of professional practice must be for the specialist to genuinely be interested in and believe in the necessary changes and to work together with the child to accomplish these goals (Toros & Falch-Eriksen, 2021). Support throughout rehabilitation interventions becomes a necessary precondition for success, especially as this group of children carry complex problems that generally lack easy solutions.

Complex and Variable Problems

In general, children are able to recognise the seriousness and complexity of the challenges which brought them to have the need for rehabilitation services. They are able themselves to identify the main problems that may cause referrals, such as educational difficulties, problems in establishing and maintaining social relations, learning difficulties, stealing, use of alcohol, drugs, and smoking (Saia et al., 2020).

Rehabilitation generally follows a normal progression, wherein children deny having problems in the initial phase of the process but later can become convinced that services can help. This indicates that it takes time for children to develop an understanding that their problems are real, and that they are capable of change. In order to manage the complexities and help the child become willing to begin addressing areas where they face different challenges, practitioners must allow the child to express their views and to allow the process to continue in a relevant manner, thereby strengthening the child's commitment, their identification with their path, and their sense of control of their own lives (Cashmore & Parkinson, 2009).

Although their problems are complex, children participating in rehabilitation services need simple lives and simple solutions so that they have the greatest room to process their own choices on how to change. It is to be expected that children will become tired of accusatory attitudes and the bureaucratic procedures imposed on them, and feel discouraged by the hopelessness they can perceive from the helping sector, non-systematic approaches, insufficient information exchange, and actions focused on problems rather than on building their strengths. All these challenges will decrease children's faith that positive change can be possible.

Concluding Remarks: Improving Participation for Dually Involved Children in Practice

In order for children to be motivated to receive rehabilitation services, it is key to inform the children that they have certain needs they do not necessarily want. While rehabilitation will not be their first choice, their understanding of both the value and positive impact on their lives will grow gradually (Saia et al., 2020). In order to gain trust and for the process to secure positive outcomes for the child, and to ensure that the child develops further on their own developmental trajectory, it is important for the child to be informed about the process and what is needed for a successful outcome. Professionals must also acquire and provide information about additional support and aftercare services that are readily accessible to the family, especially services close to their neighbourhood, that can assist in building healthy social networks for the child. In practice, the key factor is communication, and the motivation to participate.

Experiences where interventions had no positive outcome will make children in need of time-consuming rehabilitation feel hopeless, helpless, and suspicious of services. Children value mutually respectful and trustworthy people, open information sharing, and understanding, rather than an accusatory approach (Lauri et al., 2020; Toros et al., 2018). Children report that they want to participate (Toros & Falch-Eriksen, 2021), and dually involved children are no exception. Not only can we assume their desire to participate, but when the aim is to make sure these children's developmental trajectories are repaired, their involvement is imperative to match decisions to their potential future best interests. What decisions are made and what measures are implemented all contribute to helping the child change into a better version of themselves. Knowing that children's participation is imperative, having professionals that lack the skills and knowledge on how to empower children becomes a threat not only to the aim of practice, but to the rights of the child themselves. Services must "take all appropriate measures to promote physical and psychological recovery and social reintegration" (CRC Art. 39).

Dually involved children have the additional burden of accumulated risk factors. They are struggling in the circle of destructive relations, negative influence by friends, uncertainty about the future, failures at school, constant negative feedback, bad habits, and stigmatisation. They are aware of the complexity of their problems (Saia et al., 2020), but the lack of a coherent approach to professional and rights-based practice undercuts their needs. Practitioners must fulfil their obligation to enforce the rights of the child. These issues also speak to a larger systemic problem wherein professionals are not prepared to ensure that children's participation is all-encompassing through administrative and judicial proceedings, and that participation is a hallmark of the rehabilitation treatment itself. The aim of rights-based services is to secure the child's transition back into society where the child can develop normally on their own terms. In this sense, there is not only a need to build a smooth transition from services to independent coping, but also to ensure that this independence is a choice that is in the child's own best interests.

To improve dually involved children's participation, it is essential to be present with them (as a parent, as a friend, as a professional), to build trust during the process, to actively listen and to understand what the child's interests are, what they think, feel, how they perceive and interpret different situations and problems, and how they are empowered to seek out solutions. By securing open, safe and honest settings for communication, practitioners can acquire the knowledge needed to reflect on how practices impact different developmental trajectories for children, and what decisions need to be made with the child as an active participant, taking into account their thoughts, suggestions, fears, and needs. It is the responsibility of service professionals to create the atmosphere and the preconditions to motivate dually involved children to participate in judicial and administrative procedures, and to contribute to decision-making processes that affect their lives. Children truly being able to participate can be seen as a key turning point for creating real and long-lasting changes to improve the child's life and move their developmental trajectory away from anti-social and criminal behaviour. As participation is a core pillar of CFJ, such an approach illustrates the importance of Article 12 in REF s.

References

AIHW. (2018). *Young People in Child Protection and under Youth Justice Supervision.* https://www.aihw.gov.au/reports/child-protection/young-people-in-youth-justice-supervision-2013-17/

Archard, D., & Skivenes, M. (2009). Balancing a child's best interests and a child's views. *The International Journal of Children's Rights, 17*(1), 1–21.

Bradshaw, W., & Roseborough, D. (2005). Restorative justice dialogue: The impact of mediation and conferencing on juvenile recidivism. *Federal Probation, 69*(2). https://www.uscourts.gov/sites/default/files/fed_probation_dec_2005.pdf

Case, S., & Haines, K. (2015). Children first, offenders second: The centrality of engagement in positive youth justice. *The Howard Journal, 54*, 157–175.

Cashmore, J. (2012). The link between child maltreatment and adolescent offending: Systems neglect of adolescents. *Family Matters, 89*, 31–41.

Cashmore, J., & Parkinson, P. (2009). Children's participation in family law disputes. The views of children, parents, lawyers and counsellors. *Family Matters, 82*, 15–21.

Cederborg, A. (2015). Children's right to be heard from their unique perspectives. In S. Mahmoudi, P. Leviner, A. Kaldal & K. Lainpelto (Eds.), *Child-Friendly Justice: A Quarter of a Century of the UN Convention on the Rights of the Child* (pp. 73–84). Leiden: Brill Nijhoff.

Center for Juvenile Justice Reform at the Georgetown University. (2015). *The Cross-over Youth Practice Model (CYPM): An Abbreviated Guide.* http://cjjr.georgetown.edu/wp-content/uploads/2015/07/CYPM-Abbreviated-Guide-2015.pdf

Center for Juvenile Justice Reform at the Georgetown University. (2017). *The Cross-over Youth Practice Model (CYPM): Participating Jurisdictions.* http://cjjr.georgetown.edu/our-work/crossover-youth-practice-model

Chen, S., Matruglio, T., Weatherburn, D., & Hua, J. (2005). The transition from juvenile to adult criminal careers. *Crime and Justice Bulletin, 86,* 2–12.

CRC (United Nations Convention on the Rights of the Child). (1989). New York: United Nations.

Cullen, F.T. (2012). *Reaffirming Rehabilitation: Crisis in Criminal Justice Policy.* London: Routledge.

Ferguson, L. (2013). Not merely rights for children but children's rights: The theory gap and the assumption of the importance of children's rights. *International Journal of Children's Rights, 21,* 177–208.

Guidelines of the Committee of Ministers of the Council of Europe on Child-friendly Justice. (2010). Council of Europe Publishing. https://rm.coe.int/16804b2cf3

Herz, D.C., Ryan, J.P., & Bilchik, S. (2010). Challenges facing crossover youth: An examination of juvenile-justice decision making and recidivism. *Family Court Review, 48,* 305–321.

Hillege, S.L., Brand, E., Mulder, E.A., Vermeiren, R., & van Domburgh, L. (2017). Serious juvenile offenders: classification into subgroups based on static and dynamic characteristics. *Child and Adolescent Psychiatry and Mental Health, 11,* 67. https://doi.org/10.1186/s13034-017-0201-4

Hirsch, R., Dierkhising, C., & Herz, D. (2018). Educational risk, recidivism, and service access among youth involved in both the child welfare and juvenile justice systems. *Children and Youth Services Review, 85,* 72–80.

Hockenberry, S. (2018). Juveniles in residential placement. *OJJDP National Report Series.* Washington, DC: Department of Justice.

Hollingsworth, K. (2014). *Re-Imagining Justice for Children: A New Rights-Based Approach to Youth Justice.* https://howardleague.org/wp-content/uploads/2016/04/HLWP_10_2014.pdf

Kenny, D., & Nelson, P.K. (2008). *Young Offenders on Community Orders: Health, Welfare and Criminogenic Needs.* Sydney: Sydney University Press.

Lauri, K., Toros, K., & Lehtme, R. (2020). Participation in the child protection assessment: Voices from children in Estonia. *Child and Adolescent Social Work Journal, 38,* 211–226.

Lewis, S. (2005). Rehabilitation: Headline or footnote in the new penal policy? *Probation Journal, 52,* 119–135.

Liefaard, T. (2015). Juvenile justice from an international children's rights perspective. In E. Desmet & S. Lembrechts (Eds.), *Routledge International Handbook of Children's Rights Studies* (pp. 234–256). London: Routledge.

Loeber, R., Farrington, D.P., & Petechuk, D. (2003). Child delinquency: Early intervention and prevention. *Child Delinquency Bulletin Series.* https://www.ojp.gov/pdffiles1/ojjdp/186162.pdf

Lutz, L., Stewart, M., & Herz, D. (2010). *Crossover Youth Practice Model.* Center for Juvenile Justice Reform. http://cjjr.georgetown.edu/pdfs/cypm/cypm.pdf

Manchester Centre for Youth Studies. (2021). *Participatory Youth Practice.* https://www.mmu.ac.uk/mcys/gmyjup/pyp/

Mayall, B. (2000). The sociology of childhood in relation to children's rights. *The International Journal of Children's Rights, 8,* 243–259.

Maybin, J. (2013). Towards a sociocultural understanding of children's voice. *Language and Education, 27,* 383–397.

McFarlane, K. (2017). Care-criminalisation: The involvement of children in out-of-home care in the New South Wales criminal justice system. *Australian & New Zealand Journal of Criminology, 51,* 412–433.

Murray, J. (2019). Hearing young children's voices. *International Journal of Early Years Education, 27,* 1–5.

Nussbaum, M. (1997). Capabilities and human rights. *Fordham Law Review, 66,* 273–300.

OJJDP. (2020). *Office of Juvenile Justice Delinquency and Prevention.* Statistical briefing book. https://www.ojjdp.gov/ojstatbb/reentry_aftercare/overview.html

Rap, S. (2013). *The Participation of Juvenile Defendants in the Youth Court. A Comparative Study of Juvenile Justice Procedures in Europe.* Amsterdam: Pallas Publications.

Rap, S. (2016). A children's rights perspective on the participation of juvenile defendants in the youth court. *The International Journal of Children's Rights, 24,* 94–112.

Rotman, E. (1990). *Beyond Punishment: A New View on the Rehabilitation of Criminal Offenders.* New York: Greenwood Press.

Saame, K. (2008). *Rehabilitatsiooniteenus alaealistele õigusrikkujatele Eestis.* Tallinna Ülikool: Tallinn.

Saia, K., Toros, K., & DiNitto, D.M. (2020). Interprofessional collaboration in social rehabilitation services for dually-involved Estonian youth: Perceptions of youth, parents, and professionals. *Children and Youth Services Review, 113,* 104945.

Sandberg, K. (2018). Children's right to protection under the CRC. In A. Falch-Eriksen & E. Backe-Hansen (Eds.), *Human Rights in Child Protection* (pp. 15–38). Cham: Palgrave Macmillan.

Shoemaker, D.J. (2010). *Theories of Delinquency. An Examination of Explanations of Delinquent Behavior.* Oxford: Oxford University Press.

Snyder, H.N., & Sickmund, M. (2006). *Juvenile Offenders and Victims: 2006.* National Report. Washington, DC: U.S. Department of Justice, Office of Justice Programs. Office of Juvenile Justice and Delinquency Prevention.

Toros, K., DiNitto, D.M., & Tiko, A. (2018). Family engagement in the child welfare system: A scoping review. *Children and Youth Services Review, 88,* 598–607.

Toros, K., & Falch-Eriksen, A. (2021). Strengths-based practice in child welfare: A systematic literature review. *Journal of Child and Family Studies, 30,* 1586–1598.

Tuell, J.A., Heldman, J.K., & Wiig, J.K. (2013). *Dual Status Youth.* https://rfknrcjj.org/images/PDFs/Dual-Status-Youth-TA-Workbook-Cover.pdf

UNODC. (2018). *Introductory Handbook on the Prevention of Recidivism and the Social Integration of Offenders.* United Nations Office on Drugs and Crime. https://www.unodc.org/documents/justice-and-prison-reform/18-02303_ebook.pdf

Vandekerckhove, A., & O'Brien, K. (2013). Child-Friendly Justice: turning law into reality. *ERA Forum, 14,* 523–541. https://doi.org/10.1007/s12027-013-0323-y

Vilgats, E. (2015). *Rehabilitatsiooniteenus riskis peredele MTÜ Papaver näitel.* Tallinn: Tallinna Ülikool.

Weare, K., & Gray, G. (2003). *What Works in Developing Children's Emotional and Social Competence and Wellbeing?* London: Department for Education and Skills.

Wiig, J.K., Tuell, J.A., & Heldman, J.K. (2013). *Guidebook for Juvenile Justice and Child Welfare System Coordination and Integration.* Lancaster, MA: Robert F. Kennedy Children's Action Corps.

7 Participation of Children in Residential Care

Ingrid Sindi

During the last three decades, a new, child-centred concept of child welfare discourse has not only gained ground, but has become the settled manner of thinking. Characteristic of this view is the child as an autonomous social actor, an agent and a subject of rights. This view has also gradually replaced the view of the child as a passive object, or even as the property of parents (Doek, 2019). The view of a child as a social actor (Corsaro, 1997) and autonomous reflective subject (Frønes, 2016), using their agency by making choices and experimenting in their life environments, acquiring and interpreting language and culture through interactions, cannot be separated from the status of children as rights-holders through the UN Convention on the Rights of the Child.

The concept of the child as a social and autonomous actor, familiar in literary classics such as Huckleberry Finn and Pippi Longstocking, appeared in child substitute care practice before it became established in modern childhood research or in children's rights discourse. Janusz Korczak (1878–1942), the Polish pediatrician, pedagogue, director of the Jewish orphanage in Warsaw, writer and inspiration for the children's rights movement, actively promoted the autonomous and active role of the children he cared for and supported a stronger position of children in social life. In 1920, in his first major pedagogical writing *How to Love a Child*, he proposed a *Magna Carta Libertatis* of children's three elementary rights: the 'child's right to his death', the 'child's right to the present day' and the 'the child's right to be themselves (Korczak, 2018). The work culminates in the demand for the children's *right to respect* (Freeman, 2020). The 'child's right to death' sounds strange at first reading, but Korczak's explanation clarifies his meaning: it is the demand for children's agency and participation which is often restricted by many parents. With the other two rights, Korczak underlines his belief that children do not *become* persons but *already are* persons and have the right to their own lives. He clearly saw the child as an autonomous social actor, evidenced by his statement, 'children are not people

DOI: 10.4324/9781003150688-7

of tomorrow; they are people today'. Eichsteller (2009, p. 382) discusses how Korczak's children were 'right owners' who discussed, justified and argued about the protection and violation of their own and others' rights. In Korczak's children's home, children were seen and treated as separate beings with the inalienable right to grow into the person they were meant to be (cited by Freeman, 1996, p. 31).

Such developments, with a concept of the child that is based on the child's agency and autonomy, serve as a theoretical backdrop for how the participation of the child has found its representation in legal acts, particularly and most importantly in the CRC Article 12 (1989). Article 12 is especially important in the context of the empowerment of the child because it includes a definition and need for child participation and basic demands that should be followed when approaching the child as a holder of rights (Strömpl & Luhamaa, 2020). Article 12 is recognised as one of the most innovative and significant provisions of the CRC, not only for what it says but because it clearly recognises the child as a full human being with integrity and the right to autonomy (Freeman, 2011).

The realisation of the child's right to participate actively, and to express their views in all matters that concern them, and for those views to be given due consideration, is a clear and immediate legal obligation under the CRC (Doek, 2019; Kilkelly & Liefaard, 2019), not just as an expression of the adult's goodwill (Freeman, 2020). It also aims to promote the child's agency and autonomy (Doek, 2019) and provides children the right to participation in matters that affect their lives, as children themselves are experts on their own needs and feelings (Dixon et al., 2019) and have their own perspectives on their well-being and interests (Jenks, 1996; Mayall, 1994). The right to participation is granted to children based on their status as autonomous individuals. Most of the other rights expressed in the CRC are based on children's vulnerability – the protection rights or children's dependency on adults, and the provision rights. Thus, the changing concept and status of the child also shift from protecting the child towards a focus on supporting the child as an autonomous individual and, most importantly, respecting the child's dignity (CRC, 1989).

Residential Care

Under Article 3 of the CRC, the child has the right to such protection and care as is necessary to ensure the best interests of the child are met. When applied to children placed in residential care, Article 3 is relevant to the need to find an appropriate care setting to better provide for the best interests of the child. As the child may be the victim of serious neglect or abuse in the family setting, and to the extent that it is necessary to remove the child from their biological family, the child must receive alternative care. Article 20 of the CRC stipulates that:

> A child temporarily or permanently deprived of his or her 'family environment', or in whose own best interests cannot be allowed to remain in that environment, shall be entitled to special protection and assistance provided by the State.

One option here is the special protection and care provided in the context of residential care. I will not here delve into a deep or complex discussion of the meaning of residential care for children placed out-of-home, however, it should be noted that there are many ongoing debates about the difficulties and lack of universally accepted definitions of 'residential care' or 'institutional care' (Cantwell et al., 2012; Cantwell, 2015; Herczog, 2021), terms that have often been used interchangeably (Herczog, 2021). In line with the terminology of the UN Guidelines on alternative care, which was developed to understand how children's rights can be understood in these settings (henceforth 'Guidelines', 2010), residential care means formal care provision which replaces parental care in the context of an institutional group setting.

Residential care includes different forms of non-family-based alternative/substitute care settings, such as children's homes, substitute homes, or group homes, which can be different based on the size, length of stay and other characteristics. One of the main characteristics of residential care, as Cantwell et al. (2012) emphasise, is that all residential care should aim to provide family-like care. There also exists diversity in how residential child care is practiced internationally (Courtney & Iwaniec, 2009; Mollidor & Berridge, 2017; Šiška & Beadle-Brown, 2020). In some countries, even the distinction between foster and residential care is no longer so clearly marked, as residential care becomes more and more similar to foster care (Sindi, 2021). Although residential care is provided by the legal entity at the service provider's location and care is provided by paid staff, the care itself is more and more family-like – the facilities are smaller, siblings stay together and more or less stable staff take care of children (Francis et al., 2007; Sindi et al., 2018). Still, foster care placements are increasingly preferred, however small or family-like the residential institutions have become.

There is a general perception that foster care is superior in meeting the needs of children, especially their psychological needs and the need for an upbringing as normal as possible. We can also find discussions about the stigmatisation or negative reputation of residential care. However, residential care may be the best option for some children due to negative experiences in a family setting, in order to keep siblings together or to provide specialised care and treatment (Kendrick, 2015). Residential care is often used for children who are considered unable to live in a family, meaning their health or behaviour have been important predictors of the likelihood of a family placement proving more complicated (Mollidor & Berridge, 2017, p. 284). Although the aim of residential care is to ensure the child's needs, rights and overall well-being, there is a general concern about poor outcomes, including a high risk of social exclusion (Biehal & Wade, 1996; Courtney & Iwaniec, 2009; Kutsar & Helve, 2012). The challenge for the child substitute care system, and for residential care specifically, is to provide high-quality care based on the needs and rights of children with skilled, child-centred professionals (Mollidor & Berridge, 2017).

Rights and Residential Care

Children's rights, as outlined by the CRC, also apply to all children living in residential care. Still, some rights are especially important to highlight, considering the child's position and status in a public care context. The CRC covers three well-known dimensions of rights: protection, provision and participation rights, including a child's right to their own identity, to be consulted and taken into account, to physical integrity, access to information, freedom of speech and opinion and to challenge decisions made on their behalf (Cantwell, 1993; Doek, 2019; Lansdown, 1994). As the scope of this book is children's participation, I will focus on this particular right in the context of residential care.

The right to participation is a right of importance for the interpretation and implementation of all other rights, and especially as the right to participation stresses that children must be afforded the opportunity to express themselves in all administrative and judicial proceedings. Residential care is a form of public care that necessitates various administrative proceedings and decisions. Article 12 states that children should be able to express themselves in such proceedings according to their age and level of maturity (CRC Committee General Comment (GC) no. 12, 2009). The presumption in the CRC, therefore, is that children are capable of being involved in matters of importance to them, as elaborated on in the GC no. 12.

Once the necessity of a residential care placement has been decided, further determination has to be made as to which care setting most suits the child's needs, situation and wishes. Acknowledging these key factors is a fundamental element in decision-making which has grown with the discourse on children's rights, but is still often ignored (Cantwell, 2015). Children *desire* to express their diverse expectations, wishes and feelings regarding their placement – if they are invited to do so.

There are two main professionals in the context of child residential care: the child protective worker and the direct caregiver(s). These professionals play a central role in children's lives. The responsibility of the local government is long-term, as the local government professional (child protective worker) must ensure the child's rights and well-being before and during residential care, with a view to the child's future. The direct caregiver(s) support the child's participation in daily life. The task both of these professionals have in common is the necessity to ensure that the child's right to be heard on important matters is consistently fulfilled – to listen to the child's voice on daily and long-term issues. Thus, it can be said that the role of Article 12 across residential care is to ensure that children are listened to and heard.

Participation is seen as one of the key protective factors for vulnerable children (Diaz et al., 2018). It is emphasised that the participation of children in care, who may have been victimised, is an important step in helping the child to regain a feeling of control in their life (Leeson, 2007) as well as a sense of agency (Brady et al., 2019; Cashmore, 2002). Participation supports children's sense of identity (Sindi & Strömpl, 2019) and prevents them from becoming outsiders in their own lives (Pölkki et al., 2012). Furthermore, participation is also closely related to developing children's ability to communicate their needs, wishes and feelings effectively (Brady et al., 2019; McCarthy, 2016). Research suggests that when children in care are not heard or given a chance to participate in decisions that affect them prior to and during the provision of care, it can negatively impact their emotional well-being and future outcomes (Leeson, 2007; Mitchell et al., 2010).

Despite the importance of children's participation, a number of challenges to participatory practice have been noted in international literature. While children in care are arguably asked more than any other child to voice their wishes, needs, feelings and stories to child protection professionals and caregivers (McCarthy, 2016), paradoxically children lack opportunities to reflect on their care or influence what happens to them (Jamieson, 2017). Strömpl and Luhamaa (2020) argue that children in care are generally denied participation when it comes to making decisions in child protection removals. In practice, children typically have a say in minor decisions about their lives, but have limited possibilities to participate in activities there they could make meanings of their own life events, important people in their lives and discussions or decisions that are important to them (Sindi, 2021; Sindi & Strömpl, 2019). It can be stated that ambiguities and tensions exist regarding children's participation in the context of residential care and that the potential scope of this topic is extensive.

The Example from an Ethnographic Study in Estonia: The Need to Feel Loved

In the course of conducting an ethnographic study, I observed and interviewed staff and children in one residential institution in Estonia (Sindi, 2021). This example aims to emphasise that despite the changing position and status of the child, there are areas of children's rights which are difficult to handle in the context of residential care, such as children's fundamental need to feel loved. For background, it should be emphasised that in Estonia, residential care is, together with foster care, the most intrusive intervention the State conducts in child welfare cases and involves the child being removed from their parents or guardians. Estonia has explicitly used the CRC as a template to shape legislation with respect to children's well-being and rights. The principal act is the Child Protection Act (2014), which in accordance with the CRC (Article 12), emphasise that every child has the right to express their views independently on all issues affecting them (§5,4).

During the fieldwork, the dominant discourse of the residential care provider emphasised the importance of love, conveying the message of *a loving home for every child* (Sindi et al., 2019). However, the word 'love' was not prevalent in everyday communication and was rarely used during the observations of everyday activities in the substitute home. Nevertheless, in staff members' stories, the importance of loving care and a loving family was central. The language of loving care seemed to be a critical narrative tool that carried an important ideological function, favouring certain ways of talking in practice. In this respect, arguably, staff members reflected an organisationally preferred narrative: love is all children need or children should be provided a loving home. In that regard, the rhetoric of loving care and a loving home established its own ways and practices of 'doing loving care'. This practice of 'doing loving care' appeared in daily activities, such as preparing good meals, doing homework in the family house, teaching children, bringing children to school or kindergarten by car, organising holiday activities and so on.

All of these care activities are undoubtedly important. However, the manners in which the staff felt they were showing love were not perceived as such by the children. Based on the children's narratives, love as a notion was never used. Children talked about good care and living conditions, and they appreciated the staff who took care of them in the residential institution. Nevertheless, they pointed to formalities and contradictions which were mostly related to artificial terms. Particularly, there is a strong need for honest communication with children, in which the necessary and appropriate terms are found (read more Sindi & Strömpl, 2019). Indeed, the notion of love may have ambivalent meaning in the context of residential care or it may be difficult to understand what love means for these children.

In residential care, children's biological parents are gone, but the children's need for a loving relationship is still the same. Psychological attachment theory supports this view (Bowlby, 1953, 1969); a lack of love disturbs children's development, especially mental health. Indeed, although children are sometimes harmed by their parents, many may still feel a very close relationship or a strong sense of love for their parents, irrespective of their parent's actions. Also, children may wish regular contact with their birth family over time. Thus, the major risk here is not making the effort to deal with children's personal needs and feelings, resulting in active and agentic children becoming passive clients of public services and treated as human becomings, simply objects of socialisation. The view of the child as a social actor and children's fundamental need to feel loved leads us to the Preamble of the CRC.

The CRC's Preamble states that all children, 'for the full and harmonious development of his or her personality, should grow up in a family environment, in an atmosphere of happiness, love and understanding'. The CRC encourages questions on how the residential care and public care systems can approach these goals. In the final section, I consider how the child citizenship concept, as a defence of dignity and as a matter of citizen's rights, opens up the possibility of understanding how professionals can support children in living their lives to the fullest potential in the context of residential care. Thus, the issue of child citizenship is considered a complement to the discussion about children's need to feel loved and how these elements can be placed within the context of rights-based child residential care.

Child Citizenship in the Context of Residential Care

Citizenship is considered in this section for its usefulness in understanding the importance of rights-based residential care. A growing number of scholars have applied ideas of the child citizenship concept (Cockburn, 2013; Doek, 2008; Kilkelly & Liefaard, 2019; Liebel, 2008; Lister, 2008) to stress the importance of the rights of children who suffer due to social structures and are not taken seriously (Liebel, 2012), as well as the need to recognise the embodied, relational and lived experiences of *being* a citizen in everyday life (Kallio et al., 2020).

One of the central concerns is whether children only passively possess their rights, or whether they actually contribute and make extensive use of their rights (Liebel, 2008). In a broad sense, the starting point of child citizenship is the premise that all children have rights – children are subjects of rights as citizens. The child's citizenship starts from autonomy and dignity as characteristics of and conditions for citizenship. Habermas (2010) in this context refers to the concept of human dignity by arguing that human rights developed in response to specific violations of human dignity, emphasising the indivisibility of all categories of human rights and the belief these qualities are one and the same everywhere and for everyone. Sometimes there can be 'status-dependent dignities', where human dignity requires support for social status so that citizens can be included in a citizenship community (Habermas, 2010). From this perspective, the focus of the discussion on citizenship can be narrowed to questions of children's citizenship in the context of residential care.

The public's aim with residential care is to make sure that the child, as a citizen, receives support for harmonious development (Preamble, CRC) according to the rights that are constitutive of citizenship itself. This discussion involves turning social issues (such as residential care) into issues of respecting the autonomy and agency of the child. The only way to respect the autonomy and agency of the child is through participation. This leads us back to Article 12 of the CRC and children's rights to form and express their views and to be consulted 'in all matters that affect them', and for their views to be taken into account. Indeed, while being separated from their biological family, children may primarily need protection and good care, but only when communicating with them is it possible to understand what they might think, wish or feel about what constitutes protection or good care for them personally. Moreover, only when communicating with children it is possible to understand if and how the child feels loved. Here, it is essential to acknowledge that children's autonomy and agency is balanced by dependency, and that in most situations children are interdependent with adults or peers.

Kjørholt (2004, referring to Lee, 1998) explores how children's voices are not authentic voices spoken by independent subjects, but rather voices spoken from particular positions in the context of their relationships with others. From this point of view, children's spoken words are not the genuine expressions of autonomous subjects, but rather the child's words represent 'underlying dependencies'. A child lives their social life within relationships and fluctuates between positions of dependence and independence. While listening to the child's words, it is possible to understand who is important for a child and why, and what that child feels. Additionally, in trying to understand the 'underlying dependencies' it is hopefully possible for professionals to understand a child's needs and feelings, such as the need to be loved as well as similar emotions like the need to belong and to receive emotional support. So, only through fulfilling Article 12 and communicating with children can professionals get to know them and ensure their dignity for harmonious development.

To elaborate the discussion of citizenship in the context of residential care, the possible impact of childhood trauma should be considered (Bargeman et al., 2021). If there is sometimes the criticism that professionals working in residential care try to protect children from potential re-traumatisation and try to relieve pain they have experienced, then it also seems to be relevant to address the fact that adults do have a responsibility to avoid causing negative consequences from children's participation. Scholars (for example Kjørholt, 2004) have discussed that there is sometimes no clear and accepted concept of what causes good or harm for children, or to which area the participation can extend in children's everyday lives. Giving children rights as citizens is not unproblematic and there are critics of children's participation, as there is a danger of placing 'a heavy burden on children' by giving them too much responsibility. However, if professionals fail to ensure children's participation based on the argument of fear of re-traumatisation, then this could easily cause or increase the social exclusion of children, which rights-based residential care is supposed to counteract.

Indeed, children in residential care may not always have the psychological willingness to participate in discussions or activities, and they may not wish to participate in decision-making. Also, children may not always be ready to deal with difficult or sensitive topics regarding their own lives. For example, early childhood memories related to home, abuse, separation from their family or the first day in a substitute home are often considered difficult or sensitive topics to the extent that adults may avoid conversations about them with a child. The findings from the ethnographic study suggest that children in residential care are willing and able to actively contribute to their own well-being and development if given the opportunity, including difficult and sensitive topics (Sindi, 2021). Children respond and have their own views, interests and insights into their lives; they are ready to negotiate important topics and deal with sensitive issues as well.

For a start, the professional should provide children with activities and allow them to choose whether or not to participate. For this, children need to understand their possible choices. If one were to ask under which conditions children really can take an active role in the realisation of their rights and in being active subjects of their own well-being and development, the answer must necessarily begin with the child having choices. The practice of choice relates to the important principles of 'information as prerequisite for participation, voluntary, transparent and relevant for a child and child-friendly' as emphasised in GC 12. Communication should provide opportunities for children to think about and evaluate aspects of their life before separation, including family issues, and topics connected to love or loving relations.

All in all, the role of Article 12 in the context of residential care is to improve children's status in society and support the rights of children to develop their potential to the fullest. What is implied is the best interest principle and that children's right to express themselves feeds into decisions-making in the child's best interests. Understanding their interests by involving the child, and reaching decisions in the best interests of the child, can thus be a concept of love that is rights-based.

Conclusion

Children, while being separated from their family and placed to live in a residential substitute home, are in a vulnerable position. The first days, months or even years of living in residential homes are a time when children need attention and nurturing from adults and are dependent on adults' care. Thinking more long-term, the days, months, or years that follow this initial phase should not become a period where practices force dependency onto the children. This would result in children being treated as passive clients of public care in their childhood and their status would likely not be supported with dignity. Children's rights in this case would be limited only to the right to be protected by parents and/or by the state, who treat children paternalistically – i.e., protecting them in a manner that is intended to preserve their future well-being according to the parents or the state, but not the children.

Child citizenship starts from dignity and autonomy as necessary characteristics and preconditions. Citizenship may be actualised though ensuring Article 12 in the context of residential care through diverse activities and relationships. The empirical example presented in this chapter concluded that citizenship begins and can be developed through communication and through practice of choice. There is a particularly strong need for honest communication with children, in which the necessary and appropriate terms are found. Honest communication is a source of love or a way to perceive the child's perspective on love or loving relations. Love is in the preamble of the CRC, but today it is not natural for children to talk about love. It seems crucial that professionals (staff in residential institutions and child protection workers) invest themselves deeply in emotional involvement with children and communicate in order to truly get to know them and find out what each child feels or thinks about love.

References

Bargeman, M., Smith, S., & Wekerle, C. (2021). Trauma-informed care as a rights-based "standard of care": A critical review. *Child Abuse & Neglect, 119*(1), 104762.

Biehal, N., & Wade, J. (1996). Looking back, looking forward: Care leavers, families and change. *Children and Youth Services Review, 18*(4–5), 425–446.

Bowlby, J. (1953). *Child Care and the Growth of Love*. London: Penguin.

Bowlby, J. (1969). *Attachment. Attachment and Loss*: Vol. 1. New York: Basic Books.

Brady, B., Kennan, D., Forkan, C., Tierney, E., Jackson, R., & Holloway, R. (2019). The participation of children and young people in care: Insights from an analysis of national inspection reports in the Republic of Ireland. *Child Care in Practice, 25*(1), 22–36.

Cantwell, N. (1993). Monitoring the convention through the idea of the "3Ps". In *Eurosocial Report Series 45* (pp. 121–130). Vienna: European Centre for Social Welfare Policy and Research.

Cantwell, N. (2015). The human rights of children in context of formal alternative care. In W. Vandenhole, E. Desmet, D. Reynaert, & S. Lembrechts (Eds.), *Routledge International Handbook of Childrens' Rights Studies* (pp. 257–276). Abingdon: Routledge.

Cantwell, N., Davidson, J., Elsley, S., Milligan, I., & Quin, N. (2012). *Moving Forward: Implementing the Guidelines for Alternative Care of Children. Glasgow: Center for Excellence for Looked after Children in Scotland*. Univercity of Strathclyde.

Cashmore, J. (2002). Promoting the participation of children and young people in care. *Child Abuse and Neglect, 26*(8), 837–847.

Child Protection Act. (2014). RT I, 06.12.2014, 1.

Cockburn, T. (2013). *The Palgrave Macmillan Rethinking Children's Citizenship*. New York: Palgrave Macmillan.

Corsaro, W.A. (1997). *The Sociology of Childhood. Sociology for a New Century*. Thousand Oaks, CA: Pine Forge Press/Sage Publications Co.

Courtney, M.E., & Iwaniec, D. (2009). *Residential Care of Children: Comparative Perspectives*. Oxford: Oxford University Press.

Diaz, C., Pert, H., & Thomas, N. (2018). 'Just another person in the room': Young people's views on their participation in Child in Care Reviews. *Adoption & Fostering, 42*(4), 369–382.

Dixon, J., Ward, J., & Blower, S. (2019). "They sat and actually listened to what we think about the care system": The use of participation, consultation, peer research and co-production to raise the voices of young people in and leaving care in England. *Child Care in Practice, 25*(1), 6–21.

Doek, J. (2008). Preface, foreward. In A. Invernizzi & J. Williams (Eds.), *Children and Citizenship* (XII–XVI). Thousand Oaks, CA: Sage Publications.

Doek, J.E. (2019). The human rights of children: An introduction. In U. Kilkelly & T. Liefaard (Eds.), *International Human Rights of Children* (pp. 1–31). New York: Springer.

Eichsteller, G. (2009). Janusz Korczak – His legacy and its relevance for children's rights today. *The International Journal of Children s Rights, 17*(3), 377–391.

Francis, J., Kendrick, A., & Pösö, T. (2007). On the margin? Residential child care in Scotland and Finland, European. *Journal of Social Work*, *10*(3), 337–352.

Freeman, M. (1996). Children's education; a test case for best interests and autonomy. In R. Davie & D. Galloway (Eds.), *Listening to Children in Education* (pp. 29–49). London: David Fulton.

Freeman, M. (2011). The value and values of children's rights. In A. Invernizzi & J. Williams (Eds.), *The Human Rights of Children: From Visions to Implementation* (pp. 21–36). Farnham Burlington: Ashgate Publishing.

Freeman, M. (2020). *A Magna Carta for Children? Rethinking Children's Rights*. Cambridge: Cambridge University Press.

Frønes, I. (2016). *The Autonomous Child. Theorizing Socialization*. New York: Springer International Publishing.

Habermas, J. (2010). The concept of human dignity and the realistic utopia of human rights. *Metaphilosophy*, *41*(4), 464–480.

Herczog, M. (2021). Deinstitutionalization efforts in Europe – transition from institutional to family- and community-based services. In K. Kufeldt, B. Fallon, & B. McKenzie (Eds.), *Protecting Children: Theoretical and Practical Aspects* (pp. 370–387). Toronto: Canadian Scholars.

Jamieson, L. (2017). Children and young people's right to participate in residential care in South Africa. *The International Journal of Human Rights*, *21*(1), 89–102.

Jenks, C. (1996). *Childhood*. London: Routledge.

Kallio, K.P., Wood, B.E., & Häkli, J. (2020). Lived citizenship: Conceptualising an emerging field. *Citizenship Studies*, *24*(6), 713–729.

Kendrick, A. (2015). Residential child care. In J. Wright (Ed.), *International Encyclopedia of the Social & Behavioral Sciences* (pp. 534–539). Oxford: Elsevier Limited.

Kilkelly, U., & Liefaard, T. (Eds.) (2019). *International Human Rights of Children*. Singapore: Springer Nature.

Kjørholt, A.T. (2004). *Childhood as a Social and Symbolic Space: Discourses on Children as Social Participants in Society*. Department of Education / Norwegian Centre for Child Research Faculty of Social Sciences and Technology Management Norwegian University of Science and Technology, NTNU Trondheim.

Korczak, J. (2018). *How to Love a Child and Other Selected Works I*. London & Chicago, IL: Vallentine Mitchell.

Kutsar, D., & Helve, H. (2012). *Social Inclusion of Socially Excluded Youth: More Opportunities, Better Access and Higher Solidarity*. Policy review of the Youth Research Cluster on Social Inclusion. European Commission.

Lansdown, G. (1994). Children's rights. In B. Mayall (Ed.), *Children's Childhoods: Observed and Experienced* (pp. 33–44). London: Falmer Press.

Lee, N. (1998). Towards an immature sociology. *The Sociological Theory*, *46*(3), 458–482.

Leeson, C. (2007). My life in care: Experiences of non-participation in decision-making processes. *Child & Family Social Work*, *12*, 268–277.

Liebel, M. (2008). Citizenship from below: Children's rights and social movements. In. A. Inwernizzi & J. Williams (Eds), *Children and Citizenship* (pp. 32–44). Thousand Oaks, CA: Sage Publications.

Liebel, M. (2012). Children's Rights Contextualized, In. M.Liebel, K.Hanson, I.Saadi & W. Vandenhole (Eds), *Children's Rights from Below. Cross-Cultural Perspectives* (pp. 43–59). New York: Palgrave Macmillan.

Lister, R. (2008). Unpacking children's citizenship. In A. Invernizzi & J. Williams (Eds.), *Children and Citizenship* (pp. 9–20). Thousand Oaks, CA: Sage Publications.

Mayall, B. (1994). *Children's Childhoods: Observed and Experienced.* London: Falmer Press.

McCarthy, E. (2016). Young people in residential care, their participation and the influencing factors. *Child Care in Practice, 22*(4), 368–385.

Mitchell, M.B., Kuczynski, L., Tubbs, C.Y., & Ross, C. (2010). We care about care: Advice by children in care for children in care, foster parents and child welfare workers about the transition into foster care. *Child & Family Social Work, 15*(2), 176–185.

Mollidor, C., & Berridge, D. (2017). Residential care for children and young people: Policy and practice challenges. In P. Dolan & N. Frost (Eds.), *The Routledge Handbook of Global Child Welfare* (pp. 280–293). London and New York: Routledge.

Pölkki, P., Vornanen, R., Pursiainen, M., & Riikonen, M. (2012). Children's participation in child protection processes as experienced by foster children and social workers. *Child Care in Practice, 18*(2), 107–125.

Sindi, I. (2021). *Discursive Practices of Child Institutional Substitute Care. Experience from an Ethnographic Research in SOS Children's Village Estonia.* Tallinn: Tallinna Ülikool.

Sindi, I., & Strömpl, J. (2019). Who am I and where am I from? Substitute residential home children's insights into their lives and individual identities. *Child & Youth Services, 40*(2), 120–139.

Sindi, I., Strömpl, J., & Toros, K. (2019). The meaning of loving family home and child centred care. New developments of residential family care in SOS Children's Village Estonia. In ISCI Conference Compilations of Abstracts: *Children of the World: The Touch of Change. Theories, Policies and Practices* (pp. 83–84). Tartu: Tartu University.

Sindi, I., Strömpl, J., & Toros, K. (2018). The Estonian way of deinstitutionalisation. Staff members' perspective on residential substitute care. Experiences from an ethnography research in an Estonian SOS Children's Village. *Child & Youth Services, 39*(4), 305–332.

Šiška, J., & Beadle-Brown, J. (2020). *Report on the Transition from Institutional Care to Community Based Services in 27 EU Member States.* European Commission.

Strömpl, J., & Luhamaa, K. (2020). Child participation in child welfare removals through the looking glass: Estonian children's and professionals' perspectives compared. *Children and Youth Services Review, 118*, 105421.

The Committee on the Rights of the Children. *General comment No. 12* (2009). *The Right of the Child to be Heard.* Geneva, CRC/C/GC/12.

United Nations. (1989). *Convention on the Rights of the Child.* United Nations.

United Nations. (2009). *Guidelines for the Alternative Care of Children.* General Assembly.

8 Conclusion

Making Rights a Part of Professional Practice

Asgeir Falch-Eriksen and Karmen Toros

Human rights constitute, among other things, a modern and global post-World War II project driven by a claim to enforce cosmopolitan rights norms protecting the integrity of each person. To most, the Universal Declaration of Human Rights of 1949 constitutes the modern human rights system's foundational document. The document declares that human rights norms are developed to be carried by any human being anywhere. Still, the idea of cosmopolitan rights norms goes further back in history to the political theories of, for instance, John Locke and Immanuel Kant. However, to ensure that the atrocities of war were forever to be avoided, especially with the horrific events of the genocide and the complete disregard for individual human dignity, modern human rights are motivated to put restraints on government and those in power. World War II thereby worked as a catalyst (Morsink, 2010). Hannah Arendt spelled the need to safeguard the dignity of each person:

> …human dignity needs a new guarantee which can be found only in a new political principle, in a new law on earth, whose validity this time must comprehend the whole of humanity while its power must remain strictly limited, rooted in and controlled by newly defined territorial entities.
>
> (Arendt, 1976)

Human rights instruments have evolved and multiplied by agreeing on certain fundamental norms. Today there are numerous conventions, but which can all be interconnected to a foundational ethos espoused by the Universal Declaration and its focus on safeguarding the dignity of each person (Habermas, 2010). We could also, more in line with Jeremy Waldron, treat the different human rights instruments as collectively necessary to safeguard the dignity of each person (Waldron, 2013). Still, in this article, I will focus on the historical point of departure in the Universal Declaration and its lead focus on safeguarding the dignity of each person.

DOI: 10.4324/9781003150688-8

For a long time, the historical development of human rights was not adapted to children. However, the idea of children having rights *quo* children has historical roots dating back to the 1920s (HCHR, 2007). Not until 1989 did the UN pass the Convention on the Rights of the Child (CRC). With it, rights had become specified for children and safeguarded their dignity throughout their childhood. Into this equation stand the protection of children from violence, which is a right the children carry through CRC Art. 19. The right to protection, which is a right any child has, is a critical challenge that the signatory to the CRC, the nation-state, must secure whenever violations of this right occur through the establishment of some type of Child Protection Service (CPS) (Falch-Eriksen & Backe-Hansen, 2018):

> …protective measures should, as appropriate, include effective procedures for the establishment of social programmes to provide the necessary support for the child and for those who have the care of the child, as well as for other forms of prevention and identification, reporting, referral, investigation, treatment and follow-up of instances of child maltreatment described heretofore, and, as appropriate, for judicial involvement.
>
> (CRC, Art. 19.2)

As children carry child-specific rights of the CRC, the nation-state is obligated not only to establish some type of CPS office and to tick off the different and explicit demands set by the CRC but also to ensure that the enforcement of protection follows from the normative-legal backdrop of cosmopolitanism that is reflective of an international human rights standard (Falch-Eriksen, 2018). Said differently, those who populate the CPS must perform a type of practice that aligns with the rights of the child. Hence, the nation-state must meet the rights that children carry as individuals in a predictable manner and according to the intention of having rights altogether. Thus, a human rights standard (where one example of how to understand such a standard is provided in Chapter 3) must pervade the public services set to enforce rights when it comes to protection from violence.

A significant part of enforcing the child's rights is to uphold the interests of the child throughout the decision-making process. Professional practices are embedded in administrative proceedings that lead to these decisions. Each of the decisions must in and of themselves maintains the decision-making norm referred to as the best interest's principle, which is embedded in CRC Art. 3.1:

> In all actions concerning children, whether undertaken by public or private social welfare institutions, courts of law, administrative

authorities or legislative bodies, the best interests of the child shall be a primary consideration.

(CRC, Art. 3.1)

In brief, this implies approximating the child's self-interests through a reflexive process that qualifies the decision to uphold the best interests of the particular child (Falch-Eriksen, 2018). The child itself becomes imperative into this equation, not only who the child is objectively but also what the child says are its' interests. When the CRC is applied to the CPS, rights-based practices dictate through Art. 12.2, that the child participates in the decision-making that affects them:

> For this purpose, the child shall, in particular, be provided the opportunity to be heard in any judicial and administrative proceedings affecting the child, either directly, or through a representative or an appropriate body, in a manner consistent with the procedural rules of national law.

(CRC, Art. 12.2)

From Chapter 2, we know that children in CPS generally do not participate in their casework and do not contribute in any real sense in decision-making processes.

Art. 12.2. underlines that in matters concerning any type of public or judicial proceeding, a decision can only claim to abide by the CRC if the child is given the opportunity to let their expressions "be heard" in reaching legitimate and lawful decisions according to the CRC. This is not to be understood as a matter of being heard *per se*, but rather a specification of the purpose of Art. 12 as a right of the child to express the child's viewpoints freely. This does not imply a demand towards the enforcement of Art.12 that the child can assert opinions through speech, but rather through any means of communication that convey viewpoints.

The lack of participation of children affected by interventions by the CPS is a central concern internationally, not only in research and education but also as a challenge to the everyday operative practice by professionals on the street level. What research has shown, time and time again, is that children do not participate adequately in CPS services, and that this is so although the casework affects them, and that the solutions often are disconnected from any concern as to "why" children should participate. The sum of all the shortcomings implies a bad connection between professional practice and the human rights the CPS is obligated to enforce.

The question is if we are satisfied in continuing having CPS practices that are not guided by any human rights standard or have any way of understanding how professional practice can become driven by a human rights standard? Are we satisfied with our current status quo? Or are we ready to make principal changes that transform CPS practices to adhere to the rights that a child *de facto* and *de jure* carries, which grants them the right to participate and express their views in administrative proceedings that affect them? Are we ready to develop practices that secure participatory interaction and are both natural and meaningful for the child?

Article 12 of the CRC, and which provides the child with the freedom of expressing themselves whenever affected by administrative- and judicial proceedings, is a right that only has a real chance of being enforced if it is embedded in professional practices that adhere to a human rights standard (Falch-Eriksen et al., 2021), and which grants children a prominent place in all matters that affect them (Križ & Skivenes, 2017). The rights of a child depend on CPS becoming empowered to perform its duty to uphold the rights of the child through professional practices and that practitioners know how to enforce human rights. The focus of this book has been to explain and discuss children's right to express themselves throughout the casework of the CPS and to develop a more profound understanding of the field of practice and what is involved in professionalising the workforce through their duty to enforce the rights of the child. This concluding chapter will seek to pull the arguments together from the book chapters.

Article 12 and Professional Practice

The child's right to express their views is fundamental when inserting the child into the equation of rights-based practices of the CPS. If the child cannot speak, their views can be sought out in other ways, either through non-verbal communication or through a qualified person to speak on a child's behalf. This is especially called for if the child is very young or have disabilities that prevent them from communicating well with CPS practitioners. The aim of Art. 12 is thereby not just to have the child speak out, or to communicate for the sake of communication, but to serve a greater purpose in qualifying decision-making in administrative- and judicial proceedings to be in the child's best interests (see Chapter 3).

When a child needs protective measures from the CPS, it is because it is subjected to some level of detrimental care. The type of care has an analogue violation of the child's integrity – the larger the detriment, the larger the violation of the child's integrity. Art. 12 serves to inform the caseworker with what the child's current interests are, or can be, on the one hand, and that the child becomes involved in their casework on the other. To engage with the child, granted the child is old enough to be involved with, it is imperative to establish a relevant and informed decision-making process aligned with the rights of the child. Children's participation and best interests are not only relevant for decision-making affecting the child but are also relevant in designing decision-making procedures and professional practices for the CPS itself.

The only prerequisite for Art. 12 is for the child to have the capability to form a personal viewpoint, i.e. to have preferences. Accordingly, to abide by the rights of the child, CPS must ensure that any child capable of forming an opinion can express their views freely in all matters affecting them. The enforcement of the right is mandatory for the CPS claiming to align itself with rights-based practices, but it is also discretionary. For example, a three-year-old cannot be expected to have an informed viewpoint on its quality of care, whereas a 16-year-old will likely have one. However, this does not imply that a three-year-old child does not have relevant viewpoints; they do but on the merits of being a three years old. What seems bland for adults is important to the child. It can be food preferences, the colour of their rooms, etc.

Most decisions within the CPS are reached by caseworkers acting upon their presumptively professional use of discretion. Such decision-making constitutes predominantly *"public- and judicial proceedings"* that affects a child. Hence, nation-states claiming to enforce the CRC must design CPS practices so that children can express their views during decision-making and that their views become "heard" whenever those are relevant. This calls for rights-based professionalisation of both techniques of practices and the design of decision-making procedures that ensure that discretion is performed in a non-discriminatory manner as possible, independent from the different personal capacities of the caseworkers.

A further demand towards CPS casework claiming to be rights-based is that decisions must be reached having the individual child's best interests in front of them as a primary consideration (cf. CRC Art. 3.1). To qualify decisions in the child's best interests, the child's own opinions and preferences become imperative. Thus, Art. 12 has become a cornerstone of the CRC and a hallmark for any practice claiming to abide by the rights of the child (Bennouna et al., 2017). Not only does Art. 12 point towards upholding the individual integrity of the child in front of the caseworker, but it also alludes to the need for caseworkers to include the child correctly according to age and maturity across the variety of practices within the CPS.

Rights-Based Professional Practice

A core idea for enforcing rights-based practices is to let go of the idea that adequate solutions in each CPS case can be directed top-down, that it can be regulated in detail, or that maxims of efficiency and goal attainment can be introduced without first ensuring they align with a human rights ethos. Decision-making that follows guidelines and routines must always be allowed to have a human rights priority, namely, that they not only do not work contrary to the child's rights but actively promote their rights. It is even necessary to understand how each child is met on their own merits, i.e. through each child's care context, and from the point of view of the child's own claim on protection. Hence, guidelines or routines must secure each child's legal claim adequately in each case as a matter of right. No level of regulation can pierce through the complexity of the casework of each case, and the need to apply specific knowledge to protect a child and secure the child's further development is called upon. In modern complex nation-states, this alludes to the street-level professionals' use of discretion, or decisional autonomy, where decisions are reached drawing on knowledge and a normative idea of best practices. In CPS and rights-based practices, a human rights ethos, or standard, provides the substantive content to the normativity of best practices. It has thus become increasingly necessary to delegate authority down to professional caseworkers on street level and their use of discretion in each case (Lipsky, 2010; Molander et al., 2012; Rothstein, 1998). Rights-based professional practice allows CPS practices to be guided and developed according to a human rights standard. Not only legal demands towards practice emanate, but also where the human rights ethos is supposed to guide the choice of types of knowledge-based practices about what can and cannot be applied. In this way, professional decision-makers can conduct decision-making tailored to fit the needs according to the individual child's rights claim (Falch-Eriksen, 2018).

To tailor decision-making to fit the child's needs is typically known as the exercise of discretion. Discretion is a three-part decision-making process (see Molander, 2016). The respective professionals across practices within the CPS must (1) define what constitutes a problem or challenge to the care context the child currently is in. This is the situational definition referred to as *care-diagnostics* in CPS terms. To compare, we can draw lessons from medicine and understand a patient's situation through a medical diagnosis. In parallel, we can draw on the jurist, who needs to understand the client's situation, i.e., the client's case. Any profession conducting discretion needs to define the situation at hand before acting on it. Conducting care diagnostics involves understanding whether the child's claim to need protection is valid or not. When entering the care context, knowing whether or not the child requires protection can become an issue that involves the child. In some instances, like abuse, no CPS practitioner needs to involve the child before enacting an emergency care order. Still, in cases where it is a matter of arguing for a care order due to parental incompetence or milder situations where the needs can be alleviated through in-home measures, the CPS professionals must involve the child to understand the care context.

For any professional, the next step (2) is to provide an independent evaluation of what is required to solve the problem or challenge that has been unravelled through care diagnostics. The independent assessment is where the professional draws on knowledge regarding what to do. The care situation the child lives in thereby activates different types of knowledge, and which the professional taps into to resonate more clearly to reach a professional decision. The knowledge corpus of each professional can be constructed by knowledge through experience, scientific knowledge, skills-based knowledge and so on. One additional source of knowledge, imperative to rights-based practices, is what the child expresses by communicating with the professionals within the CPS. If we utilise the human rights standard, we know that whatever the professional decides on doing must be in the child's best interests. Hence, the knowledge is drawn on, and how a decision is qualified must work towards that end (Falch-Eriksen, 2018). A care context can call for a child's need for a different family altogether, intensive institutional care or that the parents need assistance to provide adequate care. The professionals thereby use the child's expressions to qualify a decision to meet the standard of the child's best interests.

The third step (3) is to reach the decision itself. On a general level, CPS decisions, behaviour, and actions have important implications for the life and welfare of children and families. The professionals play a crucial role in carrying out the goals of the nation-state to uphold the rights of its citizens. According to rights-based practices, the professionals working in the CPS become a precondition for children's rights to be enforced.

Child Participation – Some Key Notions

In the following, we will summarise the most important lessons learned regarding the participation of children in CPS across Chapters 4–7 and discuss implications for practice – how to facilitate meaningful participation, upholding Article 12 and enforcing participation rights by CPS professionals.

The Meaning of the Rights-Based Practice

Throughout the chapters, each of the contributors has discussed the concept of child participation and how it can be operationalised across different circumstances confronting the professional social worker of the CPS. Each chapter has taken the child's participation as a fundamental human right and accordingly utilised the right as a point of departure for understanding how practices must enforce the right according to the intent of the right, i.e. according to a human rights standard.

For instance, Neumann discusses safeguarding the child's right to express itself in matters that affect it and that the child's best interests are a core aim to realise in decision-making according to the human rights standard (Chapter 5). All the chapters discuss participation and the child's involvement in decision-making processes and that participation is a pre-requisite to qualifying a decision to be in the child's *best interest*. As Toros establishes in Chapter 2, the child's best interests can only become a fea-sible decision-making trait if the decision is developed together with the child. Furthermore, the argument of giving a voice to a child and hearing the child is consistent with professional values the social work profession claim to uphold. Although also underlined in Chapter 3, Sindi (Chapter 7) elaborates on the central focal point of decision-making being the child's agency and integrity, serving not only as a theoretical backdrop of child participation but a direct claim to practice.

Studies with children presented in this book (Chapters 2 and 4) bring out the practice that children are not being listened to or encouraged to express views but rather that their views are ignored. As the UN General Comment No. 12 on the CRC stipulates, simply hearing what a child says is insufficient (Chapter 2). This leads to the demand for *meaningful partici-pation*. In Chapter 2, Toros describes models of participation, summarising that participation is considered as interaction/dialogue and influence and as an ongoing process as long as a child is in the administrative system of the CPS. In practice, meaningful participation is recognised to facilitate children's trust in professionals and the CPS and are familiar and prepared for decision-making. Both Chapters 2 and 3 conclude that despite exist-ing models and every child having the right to meaningful participation, achieving this is challenging to implement in practice. In Chapter 5, Neu-mann argues that within today's practice in CPS, "child's right to partic-ipation and the child's best interests is at risk of becoming instrumental".

Toros and Lehtme (Chapter 4) and Sindi (Chapter 7) explain child participation in terms of *a child-centred approach*, encouraging practition-ers to shift their thinking to child protection discourse, seeing the child as an active expert of their life and their unique situation and needs. Saia (Chapter 6) examines the child-centred perspective as a child-friendly jus-tice concept in her chapter, specifically, making the justice process friendly and adapting it to children and where children's needs cannot be under-stood in any meaningful manner without their active participation.

Meaningful Worker-Child Relationships

Creating the necessary conditions and meaningful and secure relationships to support children's participation is central to building reflexive communication with the child. Only by establishing participation that includes the child into a space of deliberation can the expressions the child comes with entering communicatively into the decision-making process performed by the professional. By equipping the child with the ability to communicate optimally, the CPS caseworker can acquire the relevant expressions needed to reach decisions in the child's best interests. As Toros and Lehtme (Chapter 4) explain, a safe environment facilitates children's engagement in the assessment processes. These authors discuss the relationship-based partnership, emphasising the sincere interests of the child and their story. Children in their study acknowledged genuine interests as a precondition to a trusting relationship with the professional practitioner. Children in Saia's study (Chapter 6) found that, in general, children had no empowering relationships. At the same time, the quality of the relationship between the professional practitioner and the child is imperative for determining the child's best interest. Sindi (Chapter 7) elaborates here that understanding the child's needs and feelings is related to listening to children, which can be achieved through communication only. Similar thoughts are shared in Chapter 5 by Neumann, whereas Neumann moves further and reflects that "the relational aspects are displaced by an instrumental application of the rights of the child".

Together with the Child

All authors state that understanding a child's needs requires hearing the child and working with the child throughout CPS casework. It is not enough only to include a child passively (Chapter 2), but to provide an opportunity to have the child have a say in decisions that can profoundly affect their lives and take their voices, wishes, and concerns, seriously (Chapter 4), similarly, as well as in Chapter 3, Sindi strongly underlines the relevance of the opportunity for the child to express itself in *all* administrative- and judicial proceedings with an emphasis on "all" (Chapter 7). Neumann outlines exploring together with the child instead of making decisions before talking to them. Furthermore, the child has a right, but not an obligation to express their views (Chapter 5). Nevertheless, vulnerable children, especially children in residential care (Chapter 6) and children in the juvenile system (Chapter 5) have fewer opportunities in working together with the practitioners due to their complex situation.

Child Welfare Professionals' Role in Enforcing Participation Right

Authors of Chapters 3–7 argue that practitioners in CPS have a central role in fulfilling children's participatory rights. In residential child care, in addition to CPS professionals role to enforce the right to participate, those who work as direct caregivers also have a central role in engaging children to participate in processes and decisions regarding their daily lives. Chapter 4 argues that regular legislation cannot implement practices adequately alone but that rights depend on professionals tailoring decision-making to fit the child's needs. Thus, the CPS professional must know how and when to enforce Art. 12 of the CRC. Toros and Lehtme (Chapter 4) argue that every CPS professional can enhance a child's participation from the get-go of first contact by simply listening to and hearing the child actively.

Toros (Chapter 2) discusses the approach to practice, or rather the lack of approach, as one of the possible explanations for the absence of children participating in CPS decision-making, where the professional instead seeks' to protect children from harmful memories or uncomfortable discussions. Another explanation is provided by Neumann (Chapter 5) and Toros and Lehtme (Chapter 4), which instead leans towards managerialism, which has created an overly proceduralist workforce leading to bureaucratic practices with low-level flexibility and lack of room for professional discretion. Furthermore, in Chapter 2, Toros poses a question, whether participation of children is not encouraged due to a lack of understanding of what child participation truly entails. This is also illuminated in the theoretical outline of Chapter 3. We believe this is a critical question child welfare professionals should ask for themselves and reflect on the values and approaches related to child participation, namely, ask, "have I done my best to enable the child to express his or her voice meaningfully"? And, "have I given him or her the chance to participate in a supportive environment with the sincere interest of listening to what he or she expresses"? Sindi (Chapter 7) similarly identifies ambiguities and tensions regarding understanding children's participation in residential care.

The Use of Tools and Methods

In their chapters, Neumann (Chapter 5) and Toros and Lehtme (Chapter 4) emphasise the need for methods and tools to enable CPS professionals to build collaborative relationships with children and support children's voices to be heard. Sindi (Chapter 7) outlines an essential thought here – providing hildren with the choice in terms of activities and choice for children to participate or not to participate. Furthermore, Neumann (Chapter 5) elaborates on the idea of the structural preconditions for professional practice. Professionals require the support of their agencies for developing an organisational design that fosters rights-based CPS practices, including methods and tools. Toros and Lehtme (Chapter 4) refer to a practice model, the Signs of Safety, setting the framework for empowerment and the child-centred approach in child protection assessments.

An Example of Active Child Participation: Active Listening through Storytelling

In the final section before the conclusion, we want to reflect on one possible method for using with children in CPS and enable them to partake in their casework actively: To tell their stories through storytelling, to be both seen, heard and understood (see Sindi, 2021). D'Amico et al. (2016) define storytelling as a participatory method to learn about a child's life experiences. Other authors similarly acknowledge this method as an excellent approach to describing experiences and fostering self-expression (Känkänen & Bardy, 2014; Tsai et al., 2011). The process of storytelling, where the child can share various themes of their life story, including important events and people, differs from the traditional child protection assessment by minimising the feeling of "being questioned" instead the focus is on listening to children's subjective experiences. Therefore, storytelling moves beyond the notion of a child as passive, but viewing the child as an active participant as referred to throughout this book or as worded in Sindi's chapter – "a reflective subject" (Chapter 7).

Furthermore, the focus on the process is similar to CPS assessments (Chapter 2). The assessment process aims to learn and understand the child's life, including protective and risk factors, strengths and resources, needs, etc. Not only does it allow us to understand the care situation, but also to co-create solutions, including the child. Chesin (1996) has outlined that most children enjoy telling stories, making this method even more feasible and where the child takes on the role of a storyteller. In today's world, with the development of information and communication technology, digital storytelling can be used as it makes it possible to re-author the story using both spoken words and pictures (Lenette et al., 2019).

Conclusion: The Reality of Rights

Professional decision-making, and the practice of discretion, is the authorisation to perform decision-making of a certain type. It is a political-legal delegation of authority regulated through democratic decision-making, and it provides the CPS decisional autonomy (Goodin, 1986). Discretion is thereby accorded to each CPS professional defined by legal rules, organisational designs, and thorough knowledge regarding what is allowed to do or not. This implies that each child's rights are a duty for CPS to accommodate. Rights create standards that each decision made by a professional must live up to and abide by.

Furthermore, it means no decision-making or CPS practice can run counter to the restrictions rights provide and the guidance they give. Discretion, then, is not a negative blank space of unrestrained freedom of choice on the part of the CPS practitioners. The delegation of authority provides freedom of judgement that is bound by the normative and political character of the delegation (Goodin, 1986). In our case, this is a human rights standard emanating from the rights of the child to preserve its dignity throughout childhood. It presupposes professional, amongst other things, knowledge and a normative theory of the professions to adequately ensure professional practice performs decision-making adequately in care contexts that are both unspecified and ambiguous (Archard & Skivenes, 2009; Molander, 2016).

This book has discussed various domains of child protection casework, assessment, follow-ups, residential care, social rehabilitation, and foster care through the lens of CRC Article 12, and empirical examples of children's voices from CPS practices are used as examples to explain theoretical perspectives. The book has also included one chapter that expounds theoretical nuts and bolts belonging to rights-based professional practice. We hope that the book will provide some guidance to future and current CPS professionals and other specialists working with children in the complex processes of including children in their work.

References

Archard, D., & Skivenes, M. (2009). Balancing a child's best interests and a child's views. *The International Journal of Children's Rights, 17*, 1.

Arendt, H. (1976). *The Origins of Totalitarianism. New Edition with Added Prefaces.* London: A Harvest Book.

Bennouna, C., Mansourian, H., & Stark, L. (2017). Ethical considerations for children's participation in data collection activities during humanitarian emergencies: A Delphi review. *Conflict and Health, 11*(1), 5.

Chesin, G.A. (1996). Storytelling and story reading. *Peabody Journal of Education, 43*(4), 212–214.

CRC. (1989). United Nations – Convention on the Rights of the Child. *Resolution 44/25 November 1989.* http://www2.ohchr.org/english/law/pdf/crc.pdf

D'Amico, M., Denov, M., Khan, F., Linds, W., & Akesson, B. (2016). Research as intervention? Exploring the health and well-being of children and youth facing global adversity through participatory visual methods. *Global Public Health, 11*, 528–545.

Falch-Eriksen, A. (2018). *Rights and Professional Practice: How to Understand Their Interconnection.* Cham: Palgrave Macmillan.

Falch-Eriksen, A., & Backe-Hansen, E. (2018). *Human Rights in Child Protection: Implications for Professional Practice and Policy* (1st ed. 2018. ed.). Cham: Palgrave Macmillan.

Falch-Eriksen, A., Toros, K., Sindi, I., & Lehtme, R. (2021). Children expressing their views in child protection casework: Current research and their rights going forward. *Child & Family Social Work*, *26*(3), 485–497.

Goodin, R. (1986). Welfare, rights and discretion. *Oxford Journal of Legal Studies*, *6*(2), 232–262.

Habermas, J. (2010). The concept of human dignity and the realistic utopia of human rights. *Metaphilosophy*, *41*(4), 464–480. doi: 10.1111/j.1467-9973.2010.01648.x

HCHR. (2007). *United Nations High Commissioner for Human Rights: Legislative History of the Convention on the Rights of the Child: Office of the United Nations High Commissioner for Human Rights*. New York: United Nations.

Känkänen, P., & Bardy, M. (2014). Life stories and arts in child welfare: Enriching communication. *Nordic Social Work Research*, *4*(1), 37–51.

Križ, K., & Skivenes, M. (2017). Child welfare workers' perceptions of children's participation: A comparative study of England, Norway and the USA (California). *Child & Family Social Work*, *22*(S2), 11–22.

Lenette, C., Brough, M., Schweitzer, R.D., Correa-Velez, I., Murray, K.S., & Vromans, L. (2019). Better than a pill': Digital storytelling as a narrative process for refugee Women. *Media Practice and Education*, *20*(1), 67–86.

Lipsky, M. (2010). *Street-Level Bureaucracy: Dilemmas of the Individual in Public Service*. New York: Russell Sage Foundation.

Molander, A. (2016). *Discretion in the Welfare State : Social Rights and Professional Judgment* (vol. 129). Abingdon, Oxon: Routledge.

Molander, A., Grimen, H., & Eriksen, E.O. (2012). Professional discretion and accountability in the Welfare State. *Journal of Applied Philosophy*, *29*(3), 214–230. doi:10.1111/j.1468-5930.2012.00564.x

Morsink, J. (2010). *The Universal Declaration of Human Rights*. Philadelphia: University of Pennsylvania Press.

Rothstein, B. (1998). *Just Institutions Matter: The Moral and Political Logic of the Universal Welfare State Theories of Institutional Design*. Cambridge: Cambridge University Press.

Sindi, I. (2021). *Discursive Practices of Child Institutional Substitute Care. Experience from an Ethnographic Research in SOS Children's Village Estonia*. Doctoral Dissertation. Tallinn: Tallinn University.

Tsai, M-K., Tseng, S-S., & Weng, J-F. (2011). A pilot study of interactive storytelling for bullying prevention education. In M. Chang, W.Y. Hwang, M.P. Chen & W. Müller (Eds.), *Edutainment Technologies. Educational Games and Virtual Reality/ Augmented Reality Applications* (pp. 497–501). Berlin, Heidelberg: Springer.

Waldron, J. (2013). Is dignity the foundation of human rights? *NYU School of Law, Public Law Research Paper* (12–73).

Index